MADE WITH

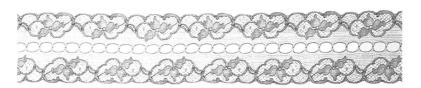

LACE

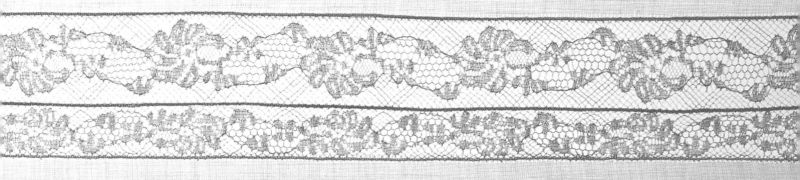

MADE WITH
LACE

40 exquisite lace garments and accessories

GINNY BARNSTON

Chilton Book Company
Radnor, Pennsylvania

A QUARTO BOOK

Copyright © 1997 Quarto Inc

ISBN 0-8019-8939-6

A CIP record for this book is available from the Library of Congress

This book was designed and produced by
Quarto Publishing plc
The Old Brewery
6 Blundell Street
London N7 9BH

Senior editor Michelle Pickering
Senior art editor Catherine Shearman
Copy editor Pat Pierce
Designer Sheila Volpe
Illustrator Kate Simunek
Photographer Hannah Lewis
Project makers Sarah Deem, Ginny Barnston, Julie Gahan
Prop buyer Miriam Hyman
Picture manager Giulia Hetherington
Editorial director Mark Dartford
Art director Moira Clinch

Typeset by Type Technique, 121A Cleveland Street, London, UK
Manufactured by Bright Arts (Singapore) Pte Ltd
Printed by Star Standard Industries (Pte) Ltd, Singapore

CONTENTS

INTRODUCTION

Think of the word lace and a wealth of images spring to mind: images of Victorian refinement, royal opulence, elegant weddings, traditional Christenings and sensual boudoir lingerie. Lace is so luxuriously versatile that it is characteristic of, and appropriate to, all these settings.

Sewing with lace is known as heirloom sewing. Although lace is often thought of as a "special" fabric and therefore difficult to sew, in reality heirloom sewing is quite simple to learn. Throughout this book I will demonstrate the versatility and ease of sewing with lace by giving both the beginner and the more advanced a broad range of techniques and projects, from Weddings and Christenings to Gifts and Clothing, plus a special Christmas section.

Each project offers guidance about materials, techniques, variations and tips, the level of difficulty, and the amount of time required to complete the project. However, bear in mind that some of the larger projects may require more hours, not because they involve using advanced techniques, but simply due to the size of the garment. So do not feel daunted by the larger projects – they are not necessarily the more difficult ones.

Before you begin sewing, read through the Basic Techniques section carefully. This comprehensive glossary of advice is organized into four categories – Materials and Equipment, General Sewing Techniques, Lace Sewing Techniques and Embroidery Techniques – to make it easy for you to refer back as necessary. Any templates that are required can be found together at the back of the book.

When you see the beautiful laces displayed on the pages which follow, I am sure that you will feel inspired to try many of the projects. I hope that you will experience the delight of working with lace, and will find, as I have, that the beauty of lace lies not only in its inherent delicacy, but also in its timeless versatility for every sewing enthusiast.

Ginny Barnston

EDGINGS

Edging laces are probably the most well known form of lace. They have been used for centuries to embellish the hems, neck and sleeve edges of garments. Although rarely seen on men's clothing nowadays, the well-dressed man of a couple of centuries ago would have worn just as much lace-edged clothing as the women of the time. The range of edging laces available is enormous. Their designs are sometimes simple but often quite complicated and fancy. They are the perfect finishing touch for accessories and will make any item of clothing look spectacular.

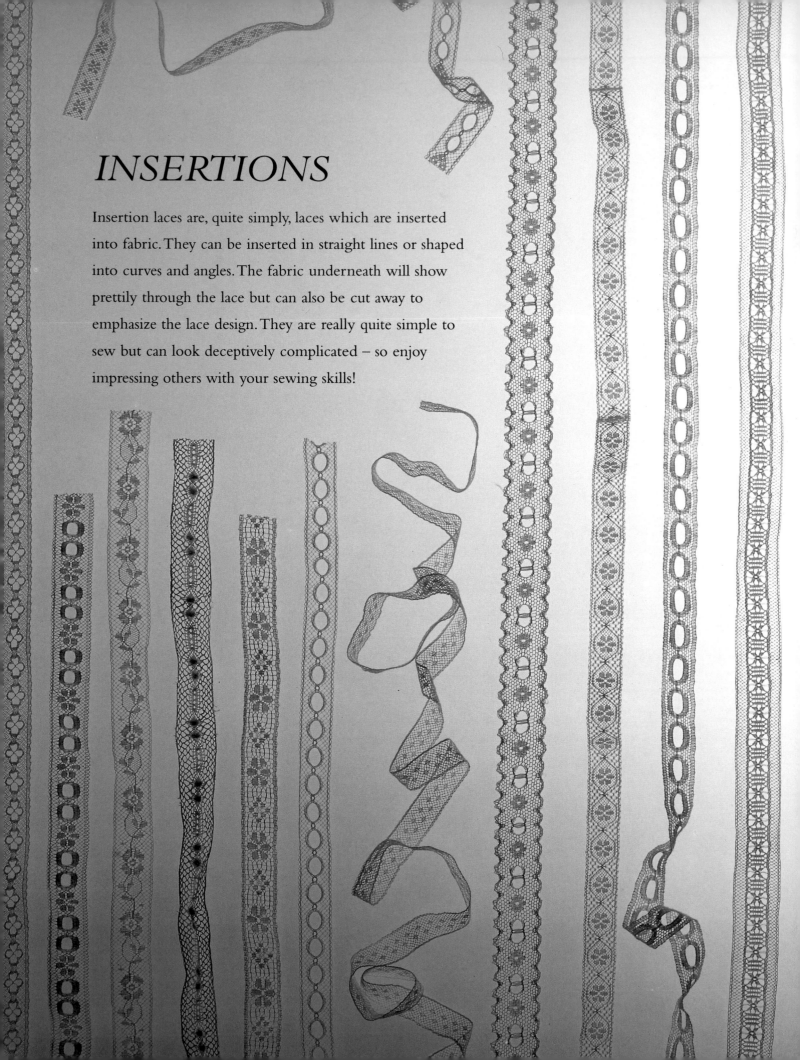

INSERTIONS

Insertion laces are, quite simply, laces which are inserted into fabric. They can be inserted in straight lines or shaped into curves and angles. The fabric underneath will show prettily through the lace but can also be cut away to emphasize the lace design. They are really quite simple to sew but can look deceptively complicated – so enjoy impressing others with your sewing skills!

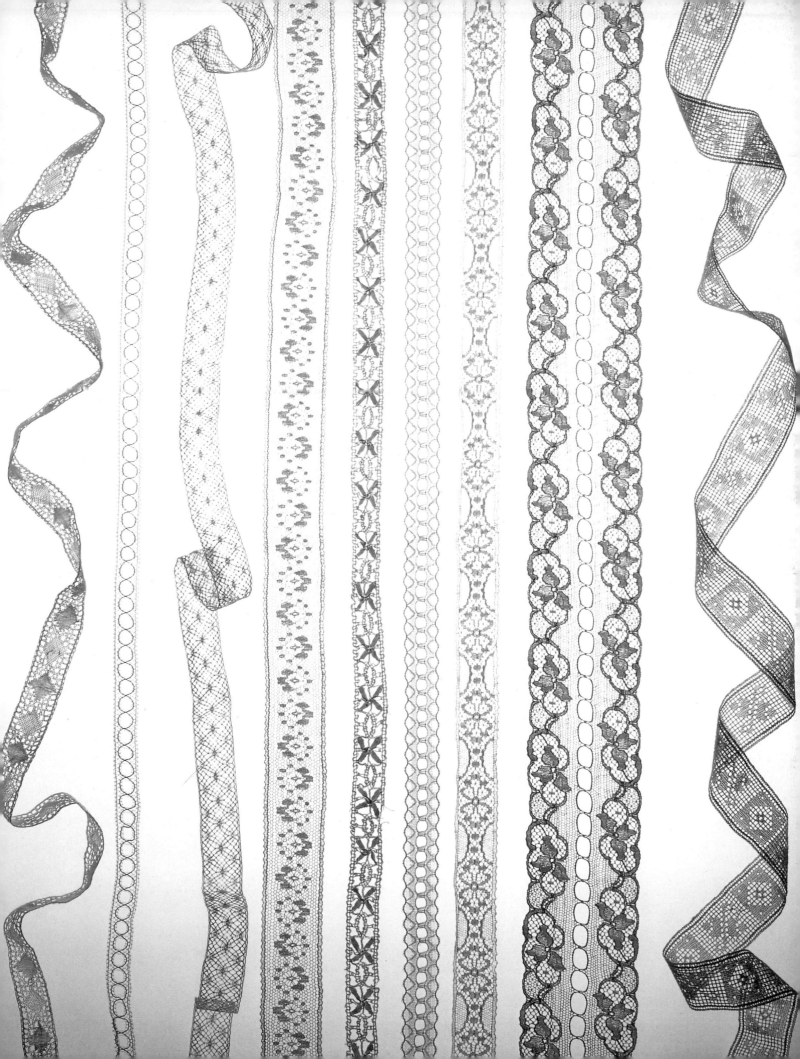

EMBROIDERIES

There are two types of embroidered lace used in this book:
Swiss embroidery and net embroidery. Net embroidery
is simply net which has a design embroidered onto it;
Swiss embroidery is fabric with an embroidered design of
"holes." Entredeux (immediately below) is a type of Swiss
embroidery which is made up of a ladder of holes.
Embroidered laces are quite beautiful and often colorful too.

MOTIFS

As well as strips of lace, there are many lace motifs used within the projects in this book. Some are quite sturdy, such as Guipure and Battenburg motifs; others are delicate and gauzy. You will also find motifs which come ready decorated with beads and sequins. It is simply a case of searching for those which you find most pleasing to the eye. Motifs are an easy way to produce the illusion of elaborate decoration and are always stunning.

BASIC TECHNIQUES

"The girls ... insisted on attaching loops and bows of silk and velvet in any situation pleasing to their taste. Gorget, gusset, basinet, cuirass, gauntlet, sleeve, all alike in the view of these feminine eyes were practicable spaces whereon to sew scraps of fluttering color"

Thomas Hardy, *The Return of the Native*

MATERIALS AND EQUIPMENT

While fine cotton laces and Swiss embroideries will produce the most authentic heirloom sewing, there are now many excellent nylon laces which will also provide beautiful results.

Insertion Lace

This has a flat edge on both sides. Each flat edge has a heading made up of four or five rows of threads without any pattern. The threads in the heading can be gently pulled so that the lace can be gathered or shaped.

Edging Lace

This has a flat edge and a curved, decorative edge and is sewn around hems, necklines and sleeves. The flat edge has a heading like that of insertion lace which can be used to gather it.

Beading Lace

This is an insertion lace which has slots through which ribbon can be threaded. Some edging laces are also available with a row of beading slots along their straight edges.

Swiss Embroidery

This is a strip of batiste fabric with a design of embroidered holes on it. It is also known as *broderie anglaise* and is available as insertion, beading and edging. The designs often feature a border of entredeux.

Entredeux

This is a Swiss embroidery which looks like a tiny ladder of embroidered holes. Along each side of the holes is a strip of batiste fabric and at the point where the batiste meets the embroidery there is a small "ditch."

Net Lace

This features embroidered patterns on a background of net and is available as insertion, beading and edging. The edging laces can be very wide so they are ideal for ruffles and flounces.

Insertion lace

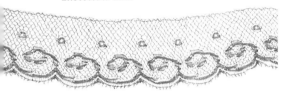

Edging lace

Beading lace

Swiss embroidery

Entredeux

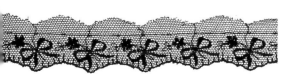

Net lace

All-Over Lace

This features a repeat pattern, often on a net background, and is bought and used in the same way as fabric. It may be made with shiny threads such as silk or rayon, or with beads and sequins decorating the design.

Guipure Lace

This is made up of a series of motifs joined by "cords" of lace. An all-over guipure will have motifs of various sizes. Guipure edging usually has a repeat of one or two motifs of different sizes. The lace cords can be cut so that the motifs can be used individually. Individual motifs are sometimes called "cut outs" or "incrustations."

Battenburg Lace

This is also known as tape lace. The tape forms the shape of the design, the parts of which are joined by threads making complementary designs.

Antique Lace

Antique laces can be rescued from old, worn-out garments but are also easy to imitate. Add 2tbsp vinegar to a cup of coffee, warm or cold. Dip the lace into it and leave for 1 minute to produce an off-white lace and 5 minutes for ecru. The vinegar helps to set the color but note that it will fade with time.

Sewing Threads

For seams that are part of the construction of the garment, match the color of the sewing thread to that of the fabric. When sewing lace to fabric, choose a color that blends with the lace. The stitching shown in the illustrations is colored black purely for clarity.

Sewing-Machine Needles

For straight and zigzag stitching when using medium-weight threads, choose a 70/10 or 80/12 universal needle. For straight and zigzag stitching when using fine cotton threads, choose a 60/8 universal needle. For making twin-needle pintucks, use a 1.6/70 twin needle.

Guipure motifs

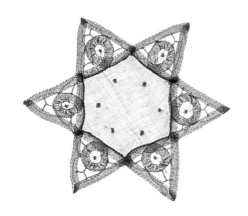

Battenburg motif

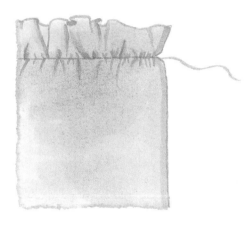

Cutting fabric on the straight of grain is necessary for all the projects in this book unless stated otherwise in the instructions.

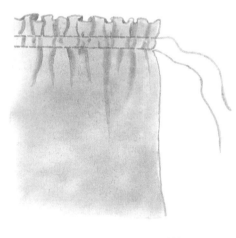

*When **gathering fabric**, use the following settings: stitch length 4.0 to 5.0.*

*When **rolling and whipping**, use the following settings: stitch length 0.5 to 1.0; stitch width 3.5 to 4.5.*

GENERAL SEWING TECHNIQUES

There is a range of general sewing techniques used throughout the projects in this book. Although lace is the focus of the various designs, these techniques are equally important if you are to produce well-finished items.

Cutting Fabric on the Straight of Grain

It is always best to straighten fabric onto the grain before cutting out any pattern pieces. Make a snip into the selvage and pull one of the cut threads. Cut the fabric along the pulled thread. If the thread breaks, pull the thread that is next to it and continue cutting. All of the projects in this book use fabric that is cut on the straight of grain unless stated otherwise.

Cutting Fabric on the Bias

Fabric cut on the bias is used when the fabric needs to be molded around a shape, most commonly for binding curved edges. Prepare the fabric by cutting it first on the straight of grain. Fold the fabric diagonally so that the straightened edge is even with, or parallel to, the selvage. Pin and press in place. Cut the fabric along the diagonal fold.

Gathering Fabric

Sew a line of long straight stitches ¼in (6mm) in from the edge of the fabric. Sew a second line ½in (12mm) in from the edge. Pull up the threads and distribute the gathers evenly. Allow 1½ times to 2 times the finished length of fabric. The finer the fabric, the more gathers you will need.

Rolling and Whipping

This is basically a zigzag stitch which can be used to finish the raw edges of fabric. Start with the needle in the left-hand position approximately ¼in (6mm) in from the raw edge of the fabric, wrong side face up. Using a close zigzag, almost like a satin stitch, sew down the edge of the fabric. The needle must go off the edge of the fabric. When it moves back onto the fabric, the fabric edge will roll over and the zigzag will enclose the raw edge.

French Seams

With the wrong sides of the fabric together, straight stitch a ¼in (6mm) seam. Trim the seam back to ⅛in (3mm). Open out the fabric and press the seam. Fold the fabric right sides together and press the seam flat. Straight stitch a second seam, enclosing the raw edges. Press the finished seam to one side.

Bias Binding

Bias binding can be bought ready-made or can be made from the fabric you are using. Because the fabric is cut on the bias, it can be shaped to fit neatly around curved edges such as necklines and sleeves. Pre-shape it by lightly pressing and steaming it into the required shape.

1. To make bias binding, cut strips of fabric on the bias measuring 1½in (4cm) wide by the required length plus ½in (12mm). Strips can be joined to make up the required length by sewing the short ends together with a narrow seam. Press the seam flat and trim off any excess fabric to keep the edges even.

2. To attach bias binding, first trim back the seam allowance on the fabric to ¼in (6mm). Turn under a ¼in (6mm) hem at one end of the bias. If the two ends of the bias do not meet, *e.g.* for a neck opening, you will need to turn under a hem at both ends. Position one long edge of the bias so that it is even with the raw edge of the fabric, right sides together. Straight stitch the bias to the fabric with a ¼in (6mm) seam.

3. Turn the bias over to the wrong side of the fabric to encase the seam and press. If the seam is curved, clip it at intervals before pressing. Slipstitch the bias in place, turning under a ¼in (6mm) hem while stitching. Overlap the ends of the bias with the hemmed end outermost and slipstitch together.

Binding with Ribbon

Trim the seam allowance on the fabric to half the width of the ribbon. Place the wrong side of the ribbon onto the right side of the fabric so that half of it protrudes beyond the fabric's raw edge. Edge stitch the ribbon in place along

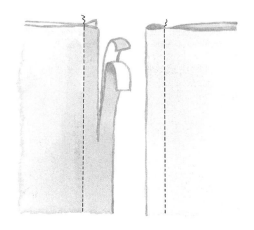

French seams should be between ¼in (6mm) and ⅛in (3mm) in depth.

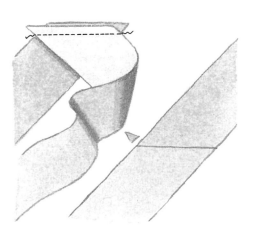

Bias binding (1) The diagonal seam should be on the straight of grain.

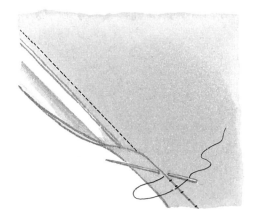

Bias binding (3) The depth of the bias binding should be even throughout its length.

the seam line. You will need to turn under the raw ends of the ribbon by
¼in (6mm) at one or both ends in the same way as for bias binding
(*see* step 2). Turn the ribbon over to the wrong side of the fabric and press.
The ribbon visible on the right side of the fabric should be of even depth
throughout its length. Slipstitch the ribbon in place. It is not necessary to turn
a hem along the ribbon's length as it is ready-bound.

Mitering Bias and Ribbon Binding

1. Attach the bias strip or ribbon as far as the corner, stitching right to the
edge of the fabric. Cut and knot the thread, remove the fabric from the
machine and continue pinning the bias or ribbon along the next side, starting
at the exact point where the diagonal fold forms the miter. Sew along this
side, taking care to stitch the inside edge of the miter. Follow the same
technique at each corner.

2. Press the bias or ribbon over the seam to encase the raw edges along all the
sides. At the corners, press and slipstitch the diagonal folds in place. Miter the
corners on the wrong side of the fabric in the same way as for the right side.

Continuous Placket

This is used to make a neat opening in a piece of fabric, such as at the center
back neckline of a blouse. It is made with a continuous strip of fabric.

1. Iron a crease to mark the position of the placket and use a pin to mark the
length. Stay stitch the V shape of the placket, starting at the top raw edge of
fabric ¼in (6mm) to the left of the crease. Narrow the distance from the
crease as you approach the tip of the V which is marked by the pin. Pivot at
this point and stitch back up the other arm, increasing the distance from the
crease so that it is symmetrical with the first line of sewing. Slash the fabric
down the crease to a couple of threads inside the pivot point.

2. Cut a strip of fabric 1½in (4cm) wide by twice the length of the placket
opening plus 1in (2.5cm). Open out the slashed edge of the placket opening

Mitering bias and ribbon binding
*Stitch up to the corners and then pin the
next side in place. Slipstitch the miters
securely on both front and back.*

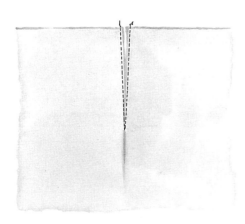

Continuous placket (1) *Start with a
stitch length of 2.5 and gradually decrease to
0.5 at the tip of the V.*

so that it lies in a straight line and pin the fabric strip on top, right sides together and raw edges even. The placket strip will be longer than the placket opening. Straight stitch the placket strip to the fabric, sewing just outside the stay-stitching line. As you approach the pivot point, decrease the stitch length and stitch as close to the raw edge as possible. To ensure that the fabric does not pucker at the pivot point, raise the presser foot and, with the needle in the down position, smooth out any creases at the stitching line before lowering the presser foot and continuing to stitch. Trim the seam and press the placket strip over the seam to encase the raw edges. Turn under a ½in (12mm) hem on the raw edge of the placket strip and slipstitch this to the seam you have just sewn.

3. Allow the fabric to return to its natural position. Fold the right-hand side of the placket back under the fabric and allow the left-hand side to extend beyond the seam. To make sure that both sides of the strip lie flat in this position, zigzag them together at the bottom of the placket following a diagonal stitching line from the outside of the placket strip to the pivot point. Knot the cut threads and weave them back into the zigzag stitching.

Tucks and Pintucks

Tucks are made by stitching folds into the fabric. They can be any depth, from a pintuck of only a couple of threads deep, to one that is 2in (5cm) deep. They are usually evenly spaced and can be pressed flat to either side.

1. At the point where you want to place your first tuck, pull a thread and fold and press the fabric along the pulled thread. Place the folded edge at the desired distance (*i.e.* the required depth of the tuck) away from the needle and straight stitch the tuck in place. To keep the needle an even distance from the folded edge while sewing, line up the fold with one of the following: *a)* the guides on the needle plate; *b)* the inside or outside edge of the presser foot; or *c)* a strip of masking tape stuck down at the correct distance.

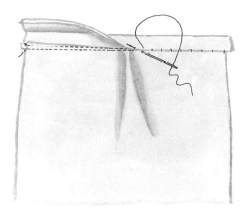

Continuous placket (2) Take care at the pivot point to avoid puckering the fabric.

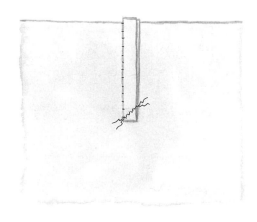

Continuous placket (3) A diagonal line of zigzags will hold the placket in position.

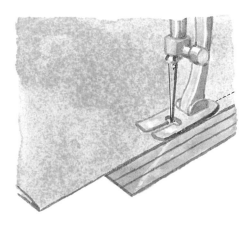

Tucks and pintucks (1)
To make sure they are straight, use fabric that is cut on the straight of grain.

Tucks and pintucks (2) *Move the needle one space to the left for ¹⁄₁₆in (1.5mm) pintucks and two spaces for ¹⁄₈in (3mm) ones.*

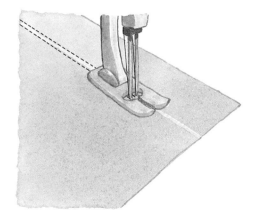

*Use a pulled thread to act as a guide for sewing the first **twin-needle pintuck**.*

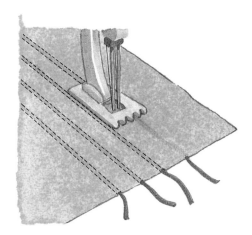

Corded twin-needle pintucks
A dark colored cord will create an effect similar to that of shadow work.

2. If using an edge stitch presser foot and a sewing machine with variable needle positions, butt the folded edge up against the bar on the presser foot and move the needle position one or two spaces to the left.

Twin-Needle Pintucks

1. Pull a thread in the same way as for standard pintucks. Position the twin needle so that it straddles the pulled thread and straight stitch the first pintuck using the pulled thread as a guide. To make subsequent pintucks, butt the edge of the presser foot up against the previous pintuck and use it as a guide to straight stitch the next one.

2. If using a pintucking foot, place one of the grooves of the foot over the first pintuck and use this as a guide to straight stitch the next pintuck. Stitch all the tucks in the same direction and tie off the sewing threads at the beginning and end of each one.

Corded Twin-Needle Pintucks

Use a pintucking foot and cotton cord such as DMC Perle No. 5 to create a raised corded pintuck. Alternatively, use six strands of ordinary embroidery thread twisted together. The cotton cord must be placed underneath the fabric and between the twin needles while the pintuck is being stitched. Some sewing machines have a hole in the needle plate through which the cord can be threaded before the fabric is positioned on top. If using a sewing machine that does not have this facility, sew the first few stitches of the pintuck and, with the twin needles in the down position, lift both the presser foot and the fabric. Thread the cotton cord under the fabric and between the twin needles, then lower the pintucking foot so that the cord is positioned in the correct groove. Use a fine crochet hook to pull the cord between the pair of needles. Straight stitch the rest of the tuck. Position any subsequent tucks in the same way as for standard twin-needle pintucks (*see* step 2) by using the grooves of the pintucking foot as guides.

LACE SEWING TECHNIQUES

The lace sewing techniques used in this book are known as heirloom sewing. They aim to reproduce the effect of Victorian and Edwardian fine handsewing using modern materials and sewing machines.

Sewing Lace to Lace

Lay the two lengths of the lace right side up and side by side under the machine foot. Sew together using a zigzag stitch. The needle should zig into the heading of one of the laces, encompassing as much of the heading as possible, and zag into the heading of the other.

*When **sewing lace to lace**, use the following settings: stitch length 0.8 to 1.0; stitch width 2.0 to 2.5.*

Sewing Lace to Fabric

1. When sewing a strip of lace onto a piece of fabric, simply lay it on top of the fabric in the correct position and zigzag along both long edges. The stitching should be just wide enough to encompass the heading of the lace.

2. When sewing a strip of lace to the edge of a piece of fabric, lay the lace on top of the fabric, right sides together and with the fabric edge protruding by about ¼in (6mm). Sew together using a wide zigzag. The needle should pierce the lace heading and zig off the edge of the fabric. As the needle zags back into the lace heading, the fabric will roll over onto the lace to make a strong finished seam. Open out and press. If the lace does not lie flat, sew a zigzag along the length of the seam on the right side of the fabric. Both the stitch length and width should be approximately 1.5 for this seam, which is particularly useful when working with narrow edging laces.

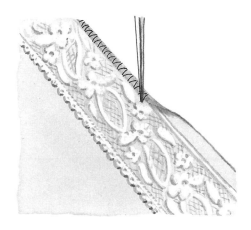

*Sewing lace to fabric (2)** Use the following settings: stitch length 0.8 to 1.0; stitch width 3.5 to 4.5.*

Sewing Lace to Entredeux

Trim off one of the fabric edges of the entredeux. Butt the trimmed edge up against the lace heading, both strips right sides up. Sew together using a zigzag. The stitch should zig into one of the holes of the entredeux and then zag into the lace heading. Experiment with the settings as they will vary according to the size of the holes in the entredeux.

*When **sewing lace to entredeux**, use the following settings: stitch length 0.8 to 1.0; stitch width 2.5 to 3.0.*

When **sewing fabric to entredeux**, use the following settings: stitch length 0.8 to 1.0; stitch width 3.5 to 4.5.

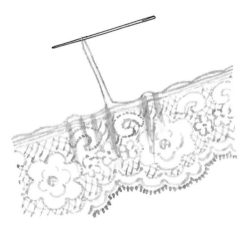

When **gathering lace**, allow 2 to 3 times the required finished length, depending on how full you want the gathers.

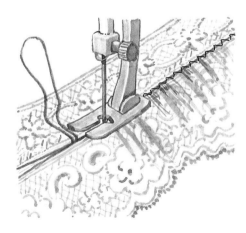

When **sewing gathered lace to flat lace**, use the following settings: stitch length 0.8 to 1.0; stitch width 2.0 to 3.0.

Sewing Fabric to Entredeux

Place the fabric and entredeux right sides together and raw edges even. Straight stitch along the ditch of the entredeux and then trim the edge of the entredeux and fabric back to about ¼in (6mm). Zigzag together. The stitch should go into the ditch of the entredeux (not into the holes) and off the edge of the fabric. Open out the fabric and press.

Gathering Lace

Use the threads in the heading of the lace to gather and shape it as required. With a pin, pull up the topmost thread of the heading (the one that loops across the top) at either end or at any point along the strip of lace. Slide the lace along this thread to gather it up and distribute the gathers evenly.

Sewing Gathered Lace to Flat Fabric

Roll and whip the raw edges of the fabric. Gather the lace and pin the gathered heading on top of the rolled and whipped seam, right sides together. Zigzag in place. The stitch length should be between 1.0 and 1.5 and the width between 2.0 and 2.5. Open out the seam and press flat.

Sewing Gathered Lace to Flat Lace

Using a pin, pull out 2 to 3in (5 to 7.5cm) of the topmost thread in the heading of the lace to be gathered at one end and tie a knot in it. Smooth the lace flat again and place the two strips of lace which are to be joined side by side and right side up under the machine foot. Zigzag together for a few stitches. Leaving the needle and presser foot in the down position, draw up the gathering thread into a loop about 8in (20cm) away from the foot. Continue zigzagging, gently feeding the gathers under the presser foot. Repeat until all of the lace is attached.

Sewing Gathered Lace to Entredeux

Trim off one of the fabric edges of the entredeux. Follow the same method as for sewing gathered lace to flat lace, making sure that the zigzag goes into the holes of the entredeux. The stitch length should be between 0.8 and 1.0 and the width between 2.0 and 3.0.

Sewing Gathered Fabric to Entredeux

Gather the fabric to the desired length. Pin the entredeux on top of the gathered fabric, right sides facing and raw edges even. Straight stitch together, stitching into the ditch of the entredeux. Trim back the excess fabric to ¼in (6mm) and zigzag the raw edges together to neaten. The stitch should zig into the ditch of the entredeux, *i.e.* into the line of straight stitching, and zag off the edge of both fabrics. As the needle swings into the entredeux ditch, it will fold the fabric edges over to create a neat finished seam. The stitch length should be between 0.8 and 1.0 and the width between 3.5 and 4.5. Open out the fabric and press flat.

Joining Entredeux Ends

Overlap the ends of the entredeux strips so that the holes sit exactly on top of each other and continue stitching along both strips. When joining ends at a corner, sew the entredeux along one side, leaving a ½in (12mm) tail of lace at each end. Overlap the tail of the next strip so that the holes sit on top of each other at the corner. Stitch and trim off any excess.

Joining Lace Ends

1. Lay the two ends of lace one on top of the other and stitch a tiny zigzag across the width of the lace from edge to edge. Try to match the pattern of the lace at the join. Trim back any excess lace close to the zigzag stitching and weave the cut threads into the zigzagged seam by hand.

2. When joining two strips of lace at a corner, allow enough lace at each end to overlap by at least the width of the lace. Lay the two ends one on top of the other and zigzag across the width of the lace along the diagonal, from the inside corner to the outside edge. This forms a neat miter. Tie off the threads by weaving them into the diagonal seam. Trim away any excess lace and press.

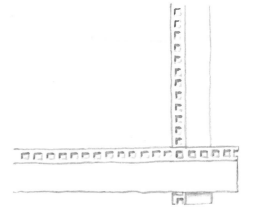

*When **joining entredeux ends** at a corner, line up the holes to create a neat join.*

Joining lace ends (2) Try to match the patterns at the corner if possible. If the lace has a curved edge, position it so that the scallop falls at the tip of the corner.

Mitering lace (1) Fold the lace away from the seam, pin at the outside edge and then fold the lace back onto itself.

Mitering lace (2) Zigzag along the diagonal fold, trim the excess lace and press the miter flat.

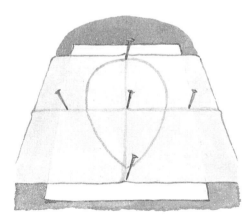

Shaping lace (1) It is important that all lines marked on the template are copied.

Mitering Lace

1. Stitch the lace up to the first corner. With the needle piercing the fabric, lift the presser foot and fold the lace away from the fabric at right angles to the seam you have just sewn. Pin the fold at the point where it meets the outer edge of the lace. Fold the lace back on itself to form a diagonal fold. Stitch along the next edge up to the next corner. Continue until all of the corners have been folded in this way.

2. Remove the pin and push the diagonal fold through to the wrong side with your finger. Fold the fabric right sides together and zigzag diagonally along each of the folds. Tie off the threads by weaving them into the diagonal seam. Trim away the excess lace and press the miter flat.

Shaping Lace

Many of the projects in this book require insertion lace to be shaped into a variety of designs. Simple shapes, such as 90° angles, can easily be done without the aid of a template (*see* Mitering Lace). However, you must use a template for more complicated shapes, such as hearts, diamonds and circles, if you are to achieve a perfectly symmetrical result. Always use glass-headed or metal pins when shaping laces as plastic ones will melt under a hot iron.

1. Trace or photocopy the template onto a piece of paper. For transparent fabrics, make the outline of the template dark enough so that it can be seen clearly through the fabric. Lay the template on a fabric or ironing board and cover with the fabric. Use the marked lines on the template to make sure that it is squarely aligned and centered underneath the fabric. Push pins through the fabric, the paper template and the fabric board, pinning the center first and then any bisecting lines.

2. If using dark or non-transparent fabrics, position the template on top of the fabric. Baste the lace shape onto the fabric. Baste through both the fabric and the template and then tear away the template when finished.

3. Shape the lace into the required design, using the template as a guide and pinning the outside edge of the lace to the template first. (See below for how to create specific shapes.) Push the pins through the lace, fabric, paper template and fabric board. The pins will stand straight up from the board.

4. Once the shaped design is complete, pin the lace shape to the fabric only, with the pins lying flat across the width of the lace. Remove the lace shape and fabric from the board and template. Starch and press the lace shape in place. Stitch around the inside and then the outside edges using a zigzag stitch which should be just wide enough to encompass the heading of the lace.

5. Cut away the fabric from behind the lace if required. Use a pair of appliqué or lace scissors to do this, *i.e.* scissors with rounded or curved, not sharp, blades. Make a straight cut down the center of the fabric behind the lace, taking care that the scissors do not pierce the lace. Trim back each edge of the fabric, holding the scissor blades almost flat against the lace. Any miters will now be revealed so that you can easily zigzag them in place securely.

Shaping Curves

Pin the outside edge of the lace into the curved shape, following the template. When finished, the inside edge will be fluted. Tease out the topmost thread from the heading and gently ease the inside edge until it lies flat. Pin the inside edge and then continue as for Steps 4 and 5 of Shaping Lace.

Shaping Circles

Start at the bottom of the circle if there is only one; start where two circles intersect if there are several. Leave a ½in (12mm) tail of lace at this point to overlap with the other end of the lace once the circular shape has been completed. Shape the outer edge of the circle, following the template, and then ease the inner curve flat as described above. Continue as for Steps 4 and 5 of Shaping Lace. Zigzag across the width of the lace to join the two ends. Trim off any excess lace at the join.

Shaping lace (4) *Move the pins outward to sew the inside edge of the lace, and then remove altogether to complete the stitching.*

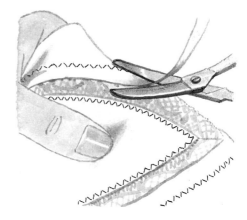

Shaping lace (5) *Cut the fabric close to, but not into, the stitching.*

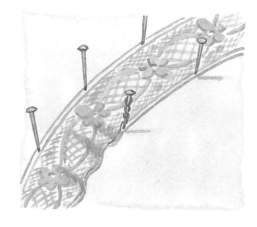

*When **shaping curves**, use a fingernail or a pin to distribute the "ease" evenly. You may find it helpful to wrap the thread temporarily around a pin to anchor it while you do this.*

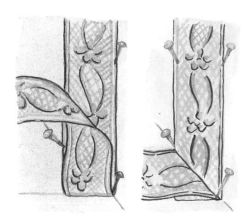

Shaping angles (miters) is used to create chevron, diamond and heart designs.

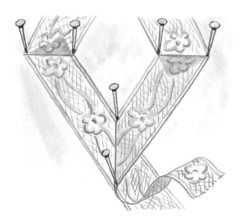

Shaping chevrons and diamonds
A diamond is more complicated than a chevron as the ends of lace must be joined at the bottom angle to form a neat miter.

Shaping hearts *combines the techniques of shaping curves and angles.*

Shaping Angles (Miters)

Shaping angles to form neat miters can be quite tricky. However, it is well worth spending some time and patience practicing this technique as the results will be well worth the effort.

1. Pin both edges of the lace into position as far as the angle that is to be mitered. Position a pin on both the inside and outside edges of the lace at this angle so that they both pierce the bisecting guideline. Fold the lace back on itself so that it lies on top of the previously pinned lace. Remove the pin on the inside edge, replacing it so that it now goes through both layers of lace. This forms the miter. Fold the lace over the miter and continue to the next corner. Continue as for Steps 4 and 5 of Shaping Lace.

2. Secure the miters by sewing along the diagonal folds of lace with a tiny zigzag. Trim off any excess lace.

Shaping Chevrons and Diamonds

A chevron has no lace joins. Start at the bottom and work upward, mitering the angles as required. For a diamond, leave a 1½in (4cm) tail of lace at the bottom angle of the shape. Complete the diamond, mitering the next three angles. When you return to the starting point, overlap and pin the inside edge of both ends of the lace. Fold the uppermost end of the lace under so that it lies on top of the first lace tail, thus creating a miter. Continue as for Steps 4 and 5 of Shaping Lace, and then zigzag the miters in place.

Shaping Hearts

Start at the bottom point of the heart, leaving a 1½in (4cm) tail of lace. Shape the first half of the heart (but do not ease the inner edge flat), miter the top point, then shape the second half. Now ease the inner curves to make the lace lie flat, one half at a time. Miter the bottom point of the heart in the same way as for a diamond. Continue as for Steps 4 and 5 of Shaping Lace and then zigzag the miters in place.

EMBROIDERY TECHNIQUES

Embroidery designs can be very effective when used with heirloom sewing and they are particularly good for adding a touch of subtle color.

Transferring Designs to Fabric

When using pastel or white fabrics, trace or photocopy the design onto a piece of paper. It should be dark enough so that it can be clearly seen through the fabric. Position the design underneath the fabric, making sure that it is squarely aligned and centered. Lightly trace the design onto the fabric using a 2H or 3H pencil. Pencil lines will wash out, but if you are using fabrics that cannot be washed or non-transparent fabrics, baste the design onto the fabric.

Stem Stitch

This stitch creates effective outlines. Make a row of small, even stitches on a diagonal slant across the outline, piercing the fabric just below the line and emerging just above the line. Keep the thread below the needle so that each stitch partly overlaps the previous one.

Lazy Daisy Stitch

Bring the needle to the right side of the fabric and make a loop with the thread. Push the needle back into the fabric very close to where it came through first. Bring the thread up again inside the loop. Draw the thread up gently so that the loop lies flat across the fabric. Make a small stitch through the fabric to hold down the tip of the loop and tie off.

French Knots

Bring the thread through from the back of the fabric after securing it with a couple of back stitches. Hold the needle horizontally and wrap the thread around the end of it twice. Push the wraps down toward the eye of the needle. Pull the needle and thread through the wraps. Still holding the wraps firmly, push the needle through to the back of the fabric, one or two threads away from where it first came through. Tie off.

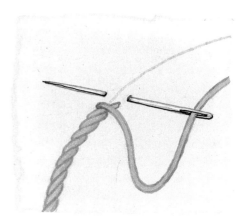

Stem stitch can be used to create curved or straight outlines.

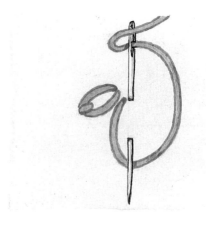

Bring the needle back up inside of the loop and secure the tip of the loop with a tiny stitch to complete the *lazy daisy stitch*.

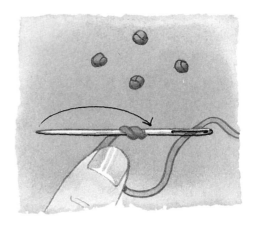

French knots are made by two wraps around the needle.

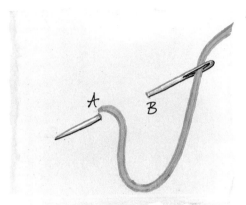

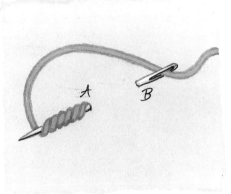

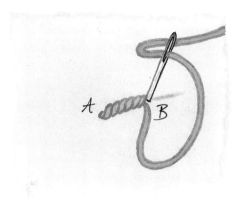

Bullion stitch (1) *For the designs used in this book, the distance between A and B is ⅛in (3mm).*

Bullion stitch (2) *The bigger the distance between points A and B, the more wraps you will need to make.*

Bullion stitch (3) *Make sure the bullion lies flat on the fabric between points A and B without puckering.*

Bullion Stitch

Bullion stitch is used in the projects in this book to create small rosebuds. They should stand out from the fabric to create a 3D effect, so take care not to flatten them with your fingers while stitching, and do not iron the bullions flat when the work is completed.

1. Secure the thread at the back of the fabric either by tying a knot in the end or by making a couple of tiny back stitches. Bring the needle through from the back of the fabric at point *A*. Push it back into the fabric at point *B* and bring it out again at point *A*. Do not pull the needle through the fabric.

2. Wrap the thread around the end of the needle as many times as required (the instructions given with each design in the *Templates* section state how many wraps to make). If the wraps are not even, adjust them on the needle with a fingernail. Hold the wraps firmly and push them down the needle close to the fabric. You may find it easier to do this if you fold the fabric around your finger so that the needle stands up at right angles to the fabric.

3. Still firmly holding the wraps, draw the needle and thread through both the fabric and the wraps. Push the needle back into the fabric at point *B* and tie off or continue to the next bullion.

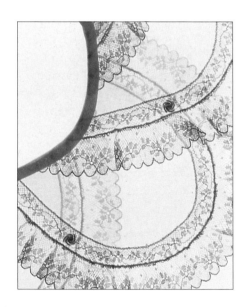

*The **Rosebud Collar** on page 92 uses tiny bullion rosebuds to highlight the design.*

Shadow work

Shadow work is used on transparent fabrics, such as voile or organdy, through which the crossed herringbone stitches on the back of the fabric can be seen. Shadow work is stitched on the right side of the fabric.

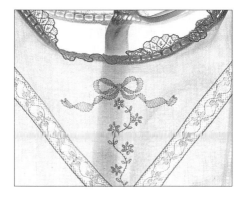

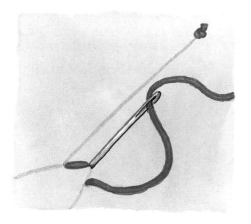

*The bodice of the **Heirloom Gown** on page 48 features a shadow work ribbon bow.*

***Shadow work (1)** Make the tip of the bow look sharp by placing the second stitch a thread inside the first stitch.*

1. Start with a "waste knot." Make a knot in the end of the thread and pull the needle through the fabric from the front to the back about 5in (12cm) away from the starting point of the design. Start the design at a corner or point, such as the tip of a ribbon bow. Bring the needle through the fabric about ⅛in (3mm) above the tip of the point. Push the needle back through at the tip and then bring it out ⅛in (3mm) below the point. Put the needle back through the fabric at the tip.

2. Carry the needle across the back of the fabric and push it through at the top edge of the design, ⅛in (3mm) along from the start of the first stitch. Make a back stitch across to the start of the first stitch on the front of the fabric. Carry the thread across the back of the fabric to the bottom edge of the design, ⅛in (3mm) along from the start of the second stitch. Pull the thread through the fabric at this point and then across to the start of the second stitch on the front of the fabric. Continue in this manner until the whole of the shape has been filled in. Tie off the threads and the waste knot by weaving them into the small stitches outlining the design on the back of the fabric.

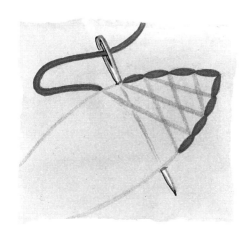

***Shadow work (2)** The crossed stitches on the wrong side of the fabric create the effect of a second fabric layer.*

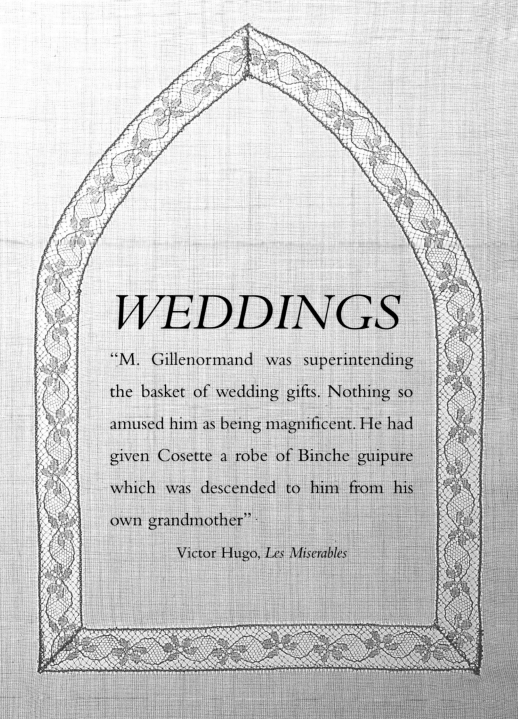

WEDDINGS

"M. Gillenormand was superintending the basket of wedding gifts. Nothing so amused him as being magnificent. He had given Cosette a robe of Binche guipure which was descended to him from his own grandmother"

Victor Hugo, *Les Miserables*

BRIDE'S GARTER

*This elegant wedding garter in blue satin and ivory
antique lace is wonderfully easy to make. The rosette
embellishment is reminiscent of Victorian lace flounces.*

Materials

- *1½yds (1.4m) of 1in (2.5cm) wide cornflower blue satin ribbon*
- *2yds (1.8m) of ⅛in (3mm) wide cornflower blue satin ribbon*
- *1yd (1m) of 6in (15cm) wide ivory or off-white antique net edging lace*
- *¾in (2cm) wide white elastic to fit comfortably around the thigh*
- *Small mother-of-pearl button*

Skill Level

Easy, 3 hours

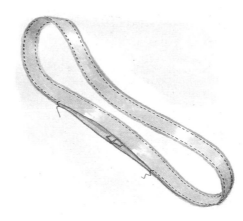

1 Cut the length of 1in (2.5cm) wide blue ribbon in half. Sew the ends of each half together with a ½in (12mm) seam allowance, thus making two circles of ribbon. Press the seams open and place one circle inside of the other, wrong sides facing. Straight stitch the two circles together along the top and bottom edges, leaving a 4in (10cm) opening along the bottom edge.

2 Thread the elastic through the opening in the ribbon, taking care not to twist it. Stitch the ends of the elastic together with an overlap of 1in (2.5cm). Stitch the ribbon opening closed.

3 Roll and whip the ends of the net edging lace together to form a circle, making sure that the pattern around the bottom matches. Place the circle of lace inside the circle of ribbon, right side facing inward. Make sure that the decorative edge of the lace hangs down evenly below

the ribbon. Fold the other edge over to the outside of the ribbon circle. This unpatterned edge of the lace will also hang below the ribbon but will be trimmed later. The lace should now completely encase the ribbon. Try to align the seams on the ribbon and lace circles.

4 Straight stitch the net lace together just below the bottom edge of the ribbon. Sew a second line of straight stitching ¼in (6mm) below the first line. Carefully trim off the excess unpatterned lace below the second line of stitching and turn the garter the other way out.

5 Use the trimmed piece of net lace to make a rosette. Sew a row of gathering stitches ¼in (6mm) in along one long edge. Draw up the gathering thread so that the lace forms a small rosette and back stitch the gathers firmly. Stitch the lace rosette to the garter at the seam line.

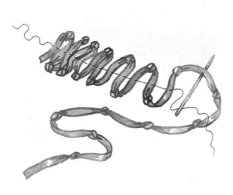

6 To make the knotted ribbon rosette, cut a 52in (1.3m) length of ¹/₈in (3mm) wide blue ribbon. Tie 25 knots at 2in (5cm) intervals along the length of the ribbon. Run a length of thread through the ribbon, positioning the needle halfway between each of the knots. Draw up the thread, thus forming the loops of the rosette. Secure the rosette with back stitches and add a few knotted pieces of ribbon of varying lengths to form the tails. Attach the ribbon rosette to the center of the lace rosette and to the garter with the mother-of-pearl button.

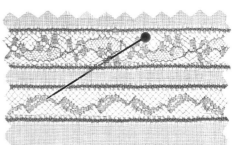

Variations & Tips
• Instead of decorating the ribbon rosette with knots, use pearl beads at 2in (5cm) intervals.
• Use a gold charm such as a horseshoe or heart, instead of a mother-of-pearl button.

RING PILLOW

A heart of lace embroidered with the bride and groom's names and the wedding date is the centerpiece of this ring pillow. It makes a perfect memento of the wedding day.

Materials

- *10in (25cm) square of white Swiss batiste or voile*
- *¾yd (70cm) of ½in (12mm) wide white insertion lace*
- *2yds (1.8m) of 1in (2.5cm) wide white edging lace*
- *1yd (1m) of ¼in (6mm) wide blue silk ribbon*
- *Dark blue cotton cord such as DMC Perle No. 5*
- *Embroidery threads in the following colors: DMC 334 (blue), 948 & 353 (peach), 523 (green)*

Templates

Large heart, page 118
Bow and roses embroidery design, page 121

Skill Level

Intermediate, 6–7 hours

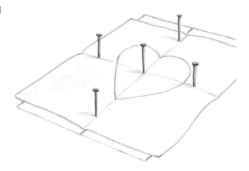

1 Find the center point of the square of Swiss batiste or voile by folding it in half lengthwise and widthwise and pressing lightly along these folds. Position the heart template centrally beneath the fabric square. Sew the insertion lace into the heart shape, cutting away the fabric from behind the lace.

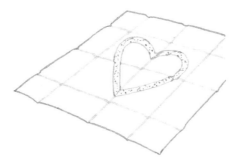

2 Measure ¼in (6mm) outward from the bottom, top and widest parts of the heart. Iron creases along these measurements. Sew a corded twin-needle pintuck along all four creases using the dark blue cord. Sew two further rows of corded pintucks outside of the first. Here, the three rows of pintucks above and below the heart extend to the edges of the fabric square. Those on either side of the heart only go as far as the top- and bottommost pintucks. Vary this corner design as desired.

3 Embroider the blue bow, and the peach and green roses design under the top dip in the heart, using the template as a guide. Embroider the names of the bride and groom and the date of the wedding underneath in stem stitch using one strand of blue embroidery thread. Make sure that both are centered.

4 Trim the fabric on all sides of the square to ⅞in (2cm) from the last row of pintucks. Roll and whip all four sides. Sew gathered edging lace around the pillow front, increasing the amount of gathers at three of the corners and mitering the lace at the fourth corner.

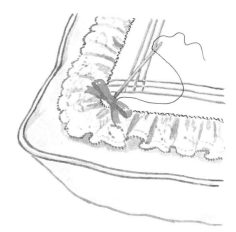

5 Lay the pillow front over a 10in (25cm) square pillow, perhaps made from the same material as the bridesmaid's purse (see page 40). The color of the pillow will show through the lace heart. Make four small bows with the blue silk ribbon and place one on each corner of the pillow front. Secure the pillow front to the pillow by tacking through the bows.

Variations & Tips

• Try using these color combinations instead of peach, green and blue – DMC 223, 224, 225 (pinks) with 936 (green), DMC 743, 744, 745 (creams & yellows) with 937 (green).

• To keep the pillow front as a permanent memento of the occasion, remove it from the pillow and mount it in a picture frame, or on the cover of the wedding photograph album.

BRIDESMAID'S PURSE AND GIFT SACHET

This purse is just right for a younger bridesmaid to keep a handkerchief in. The sachet is simply a mini-version of the purse and can be used to hold a small thank-you gift.

GIFT SACHET

Materials
- *5 × 10in (12.5 × 25cm) rectangle of peach silk douppioni*
- *1yd (1m) of 1in (2.5cm) wide white edging lace, cut into three equal lengths*
- *^{1}/3yd (30cm) of ^{1}/4in (6mm) wide white edging lace*
- *^{1}/3yd (30cm) of ^{1}/2in (12mm) wide white beading lace*
- *^{1}/3yd (30cm) of ^{1}/8in (3mm) wide peach satin ribbon*
- *Fray Check or similar product*
- *Water soluble marker pen*

Skill Level
Easy, 1 hour

PURSE

Materials
- *^{3}/4yd (70cm) of 45in (115cm) wide peach silk douppioni*
- *8yds (7m) of 1in (2.5cm) wide white edging lace*
- *^{3}/4yd (70cm) of small pearl beading-by-the-yard*
- *^{3}/4yd (70cm) of ^{1}/4in (6mm) wide peach satin ribbon*
- *Batting*
- *Piece of cardboard*
- *Quilting thread*
- *Fray Check or similar product*
- *Water soluble marker pen*

Skill Level
Easy, 4 hours

GIFT SACHET

1 Seal the edges of the silk rectangle with Fray Check and allow to dry. Draw a line with the marker pen 2in (5cm) down from the 10in (25cm) edge of the silk rectangle. Leaving a ^{1}/2in (12mm) tail of lace and starting ^{3}/8in (1cm) in from the edge of the silk, sew a gathered strip of 1in (2.5cm) wide edging lace along the drawn line. Finish stitching ^{3}/8in (1cm) in from the other edge, again leaving a ^{1}/2in (12mm) tail of lace. Sew a further two rows of gathered edging lace to the silk, allowing each one to overlap the one below slightly.

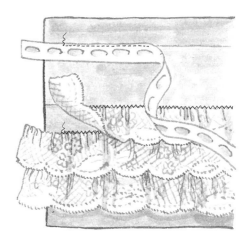

2 Measure ^{3}/4in (2cm) down from the 10in (25cm) edge of the silk rectangle and draw a line with the marker pen. Leaving a ^{1}/2in (12mm) tail at either end, straight stitch the beading lace in place so that the top edge lies along the drawn line.

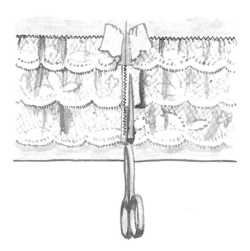

3 With right sides facing, roll and whip the sides of the silk together to make a tube. Take care not to catch the laces in this seam. Join the tails of all the laces with a tiny zigzag and trim back the excess.

4 Sew the ¹/₄in (6mm) wide edging lace along the top edge of the sachet. Turn the sachet inside out and roll and whip the bottom edges together. Thread the peach ribbon through the beading and draw it up to form a small pouch.

PURSE

1 Cut a rectangle of silk measuring 22 × 18in (56 × 46cm). Cut two silk circles with a diameter of 6¹/₂in (16.5cm). Cut two circles of cardboard and two circles of batting with a diameter of 4¹/₂in (11.5cm). Seal the edges of all the pieces of silk with Fray Check and allow to dry.

2 With right sides together, fold the rectangle of silk in half widthwise and sew together to form a tube using a ¹/₂in (12mm) seam allowance. Fold the tube in half again, wrong sides together, so that there is a double layer of fabric and iron a crease along the folded edge. The folded tube will measure 9in (23cm) in depth. Draw a line around the tube with a marker pen 2¹/₂in (6cm) down from the folded edge.

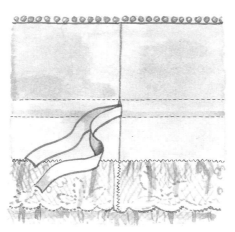

3 Cut the edging lace into eight equal lengths. Open out the folded silk tube and sew one of the lengths of edging lace along the drawn line, gathering it gently. Start at the seam and overlap the ends of the lace by ¹/₂in (12mm). Sew a further seven rows of gathered edging lace to the silk, spacing them so that each row slightly overlaps the one below it. Join the ends of the lace with a tiny zigzag and trim back the excess.

4 Fold the silk in half again and whip stitch the pearl beading-by-the-yard along the folded edge. To make the casing for the ribbon, measure 1¹/₂in (4cm) down from the folded edge and sew a line of straight stitching around the tube. Sew a second line of straight stitching ³/₈in (1cm) below the first. Unpick the side seam between the two rows of stitching on the outer layer of the tube only. Thread the peach ribbon through the casing.

5 Using quilting thread, hand sew a line of running stitches around the circumference of each of the silk circles about ¹/₂in (12mm) in from the edge. Place a circle of batting and then a circle of cardboard on the wrong side of each of the silk circles, making sure they are centered. Pull up the quilting thread so that the edges of the silk circles are drawn up to enclose the cardboard and batting. Secure the quilting thread with a couple of back stitches.

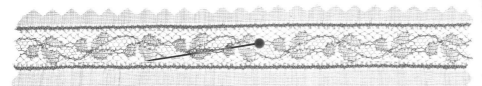

Variations & Tips

- Make several sachets at the same time by sewing lace and beading across a larger piece of fabric. Cut it into equal pieces, unpick some of the stitching on the lace at the sides, and then continue as from Step 3.
- Replace the ribbon tie with a strip of silk. Tie the ends together with a knot.

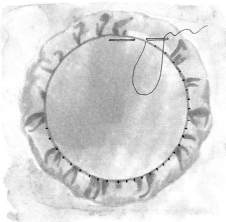

6 Sew two rows of gathering stitches around the raw edges of the silk tube. Draw them up so that the tube fits neatly inside the circumference of a silk circle. Handsew the tube firmly to the wrong side of one of the circles along the second line of gathering threads. Place the second circle inside the tube, wrong side down. The raw edges of the base of the tube will now be sandwiched between the two circles. Slip stitch the second circle in place over the first. Draw up the ribbon and the purse is ready to use.

LACE HANDKERCHIEF

All in white for the bride or embroidered in coordinating colors for the bridesmaids, this lace handkerchief is a stylish wedding accessory and a perfect gift for any occasion.

Materials

- *10½in (26.5cm) square of white Swiss batiste or lawn, or a fine white ready-made handkerchief*
- *Four 11½in (29cm) lengths of ⅛in (3mm) wide white entredeux*
- *2½yds (2.3m) of 1in (2.5cm) wide white edging lace*
- *White embroidery thread*

Skill Level

Easy, 2–3 hours

1 If using a ready-made handkerchief, remove any existing binding or edging. Even if the edges are only rolled and whipped, cut this off. The idea here is to make the lightest and most delicate handkerchief possible and so any existing edging may make it too bulky when the entredeux and edging lace are attached.

2 Sew a strip of entredeux along each side of the fabric square, neatly overlapping the holes in the entredeux at the corners.

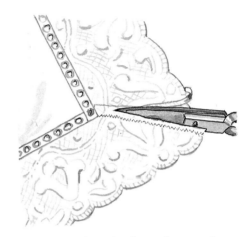

3 Sew gathered edging lace to the other side of the entredeux, increasing the amount of gathers at three of the corners and mitering the lace at the fourth corner. Sew a close zigzag along the miter and trim away any excess lace.

4 Using one strand of embroidery thread and stem stitch, sew the initial of the bride at one of the corners and add a small "flourish" design to ornament the initial.

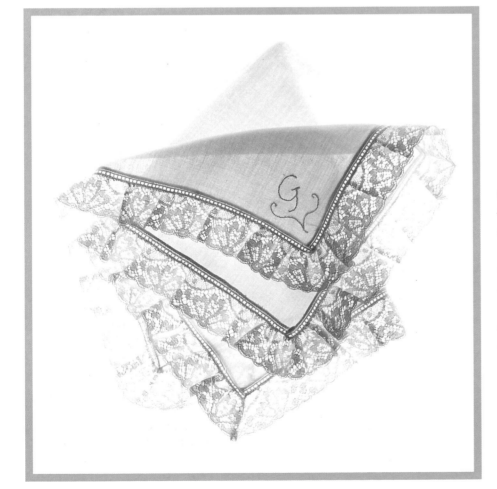

Variations & Tips

- Substitute insertion lace for the entredeux.
- Stitch a small floral embroidery design in pastel colors in one corner instead of an initial.

VICTORIAN SAMPLER

*Strips of antique lace echo the bands of letters on
traditional cross-stitch samplers and are balanced by the
simple ring design. The ribbon frame completes the picture.*

Materials
- *Strips of antique insertion laces and embroideries at least 10in (25cm) in length — the width of the laces can vary as long as there is sufficient to make a rectangle 8in (20cm) in depth when sewn together*
- *10 × 6in (25 × 15cm) rectangle of fine white cotton lawn*
- *³/₄yd (70cm) of ¹/₂in (12mm) wide white insertion lace*
- *1¹/₂yds (1.4m) of 1in (2.5cm) wide cream satin ribbon (use antique ribbon if available)*
- *Gold metallic embroidery thread*

Templates
Interlacing rings, page 118

Skill Level
Intermediate, 4–5 hours

1 Examine the antique laces and embroideries, and select those strips that are best preserved. Wash them and leave to dry. Lay out the laces and experiment with different combinations until you find the most pleasing arrangement. None of the colors of the laces will match, nor will the patterns or designs, so use your sense of taste and style to arrange them in your own way. Sew the strips together so that they form a rectangle measuring 10 × 8in (25 × 20cm).

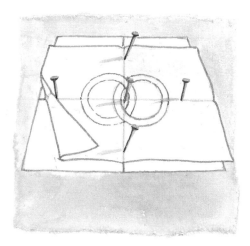

2 Find the center point of the rectangle of lawn by folding it in half lengthwise and widthwise and pressing lightly along these folds. Position the interlacing rings template underneath the fabric rectangle, lining up the creases with the center point and the cross bars marked on the template. Shape the ¹/₂in (12mm) wide insertion lace to form the two circles and sew in place, cutting away the fabric from behind the lace.

3 Using stem stitch and one strand of gold metallic embroidery thread, embroider the initials of the bride and groom inside the interlaced rings and the date of the wedding underneath. Sew the embroidered fabric to the rectangle of antique laces.

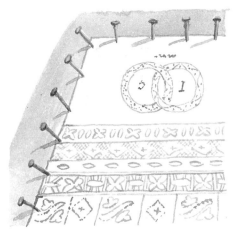

4 Dampen the sampler and then block it by pinning each of the sides out so that they lie straight and the corners are square. Allow the antique section to dry into shape naturally; steam iron the rest.

5 Pin the ribbon around the edges of the sampler, allowing the outer edge to overlap the raw edges of the lace and fabric rectangle. Miter the ribbon at the corners and straight stitch in place along the inner edge of the ribbon and along each of the miters. Block and steam the sampler again and leave it to dry before removing the pins. Mount the finished sampler on a dark colored background, such as royal blue, which will display the delicacy of the lace work to best advantage.

Variations & Tips

- Use strips of pintucked fabric and modern insertion laces if you do not have sufficient antique laces.
- Leave off the interlacing rings at the bottom of the sampler and make it completely from antique laces.

CHRISTENINGS

"People … always buy white for little new babies. … They make fine seams, and tucks, and put on lace and trimming by hand"

Gene Stratton Porter, *Freckles*

HEIRLOOM GOWN

This exquisite gown is destined to become a family heirloom which will be handed down for generations. It is truly a labor of love and deserves the finest cotton laces.

Materials

- 2¼yds (2.1m) of 45in (115cm) wide white Swiss batiste or voile
- 11yds (10m) of ³⁄₈in (1cm) wide white Swiss insertion
- 3¼yds (3m) of ½in (12mm) wide white Swiss beading
- 5¼yds (5m) of ⁵⁄₈in (1.5cm) wide white insertion lace
- 1¼yds (1.2m) of ³⁄₈in (1cm) wide white insertion lace
- 4½yds (4m) of 2in (5cm) wide white edging lace
- 1¾yds (1.6m) of ⁵⁄₈in (1.5cm) wide white edging lace
- ³⁄₄yd (70cm) of ³⁄₈in (1cm) wide white edging lace
- ³⁄₄yd (70cm) of ¼in (6mm) wide white entredeux
- 1yd (1m) of ¹⁄₈in (3mm) wide white entredeux
- 4¾yds (4.5m) of ³⁄₈in (1cm) wide white double-sided satin ribbon
- 2⅓yds (2.2m) of ¹⁄₈in (3mm) wide white double-sided satin ribbon
- White embroidery thread

Size

To fit a baby of 3–9 months

Templates

Bodice front, back and sleeves, page 119
Bow and daisies embroidery design, page 121

Skill Level

Advanced, 30–40 hours

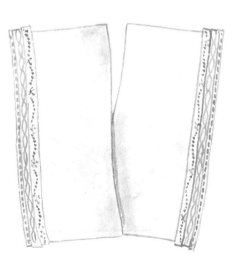

BODICE

1 Cut two strips of Swiss insertion, two strips of ³⁄₈in (1cm) wide insertion lace, and two strips of ¹⁄₈in (3mm) wide entredeux, all 7in (18cm) long. Cut two 3½ × 7in (9 × 18cm) rectangles of batiste. Sew Swiss insertion to one side of both strips of insertion lace and entredeux to the other side of them. Sew the fabric rectangles to the Swiss insertions.

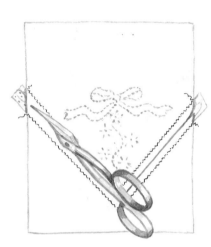

2 Cut a 6 × 7in (15 × 18cm) rectangle of fabric. This will be the central panel of the bodice front. Using the bodice front template as a guide, shape some ³⁄₈in (1cm) wide insertion lace into the V shape. Sew in place but do not cut away the fabric from behind the lace until the embroidery is completed. Trace the bow and daisies design onto the fabric, positioning it centrally above the point of the lace V, and embroider it using one strand of white embroidery thread. Cut away the fabric from behind the lace and sew down the miter.

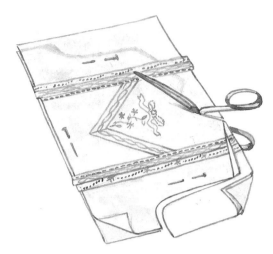

3 Join the central panel to the entredeux edges of the pieces sewn in Step 1, using $^3/_8$in (1cm) seam allowances. The finished width of the central embroidered panel is now 5$^1/_4$in (13.5cm). Pin the finished rectangle over the bodice front template, lining up the center of the rectangle with the center of the template, and cut out.

4 To make the bodice back, repeat Step 1, and then cut two rectangles of fabric 4$^1/_2$ × 7in (11.5 × 18cm). Join a fabric rectangle to the entredeux edge of each of the other two pieces. Pin the finished rectangles on the bodice back template. Cut out two backs. Remember to cut a left and a right back. To finish the center back openings, turn under $^1/_2$in (12mm) of fabric, press, then turn under along the fold line and press again. Straight stitch in place.

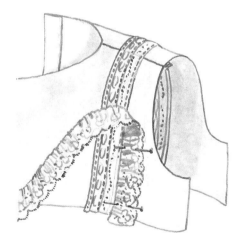

5 Join the front and back pieces at the shoulders with a French seam. Cut two 17in (43cm) strips of $^5/_8$in (1.5cm) wide edging lace. Sew it to the outer edge of the Swiss insertion, making sure the lace has plenty of gathers to ease it over the shoulder seams.

6 Sew $^1/_4$in (6mm) wide entredeux to the neck edge. To ensure that the entredeux sits flat, sew a narrow zigzag along the seam on the right side of the fabric. Sew gathered $^3/_8$in (1cm) wide edging lace to the other side of the entredeux. Leave a $^1/_2$in (12mm) tail of lace at each end. Turn it under and slip stitch in place to neaten.

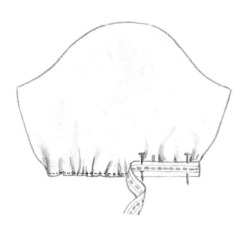

SLEEVES

7 Cut out two sleeves in fabric. Cut two 7in (18cm) strips of ¹/₄in (6mm) wide entredeux. Gather the lower edges of the sleeves and draw up the gathers to 7in (18cm). Sew the gathered sleeve edges to the entredeux. Cut two 14in (36cm) strips of ⁵/₈in (1.5cm) wide edging lace, gather them and sew them to the other sides of the entredeux around the sleeve edges.

8 Gather the upper edge of the sleeves between the points marked on the template, and then sew the sleeves to the bodice using French seams. Join the sleeve and side seams of the bodice in one continuous French seam.

9 Leaving a ¹/₂in (12mm) tail of lace at each end, sew Swiss beading around the entire lower edge of the bodice. Fold under the lace tails at the center back, matching the ribbon slots, and slip stitch in place.

SKIRT

10 To make the lace bands for the lower edge of the skirt, cut one strip of Swiss beading, four strips of Swiss insertion and two strips of ⁵/₈in (1.5cm) wide insertion lace. Each strip should be 90in (230cm) long, i.e. twice the width of the fabric. Sew a strip of Swiss insertion to each side of the insertion lace strips to make two lace bands.

11 To make the two pintuck bands, cut four 3 × 45in (7.5 × 115cm) strips of fabric. Join them together using French seams to make two 90in (2.3m) long strips. Sew the first ¹/₁₆in (2mm) wide pintuck 1in (2.5cm) down from the top edges. Sew two more pintucks ³/₈in (1cm) apart. Sew each pintuck band to one of the lace bands, and then sew the other edge of the pintuck bands to the Swiss beading. For the pintuck strips to look balanced, it is important that there is ⁵/₈in (1.5cm) of fabric between the Swiss insertion and the first pintuck and between the beading and the last pintuck. Sew gathered 2in (5cm) wide edging lace around the lower edge of this lace and pintuck panel.

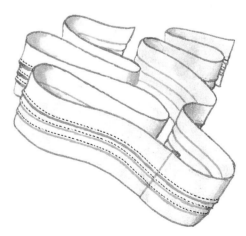

12 To make the skirt of the gown, cut two rectangles of fabric, each measuring 27 × 45in (69 × 115cm). Join them together along one of the short edges with a French seam. Sew the fabric to the upper edge of the lace and pintuck band. Join the other side of the skirt with a French seam, taking care to match up the pintucks and laces.

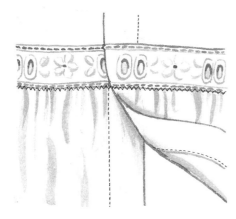

13 Cut a 7in (18cm) slit in the center back of the skirt and make a continuous placket. Gather the upper edge of the skirt and attach it to the beading on the bodice. To make this seam lie flat, stitch a narrow zigzag over the seam on the right side of the gown.

14 Thread $^1/_8$in (3mm) wide ribbon through the entredeux around the neck and sleeve edges, and $^3/_8$in (1cm) wide ribbon through the beading on the skirt and the bodice. Leave long ribbon ties at the back of the bodice.

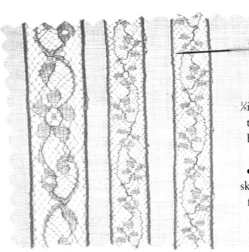

Variations & Tips
- Make ribbon rosettes from ⅛in (3mm) wide ribbon and sew these onto the beading on the bodice so that they trail down the front of the gown.
- Sew more lace bands on the skirt and adjust the length of the fabric of the skirt accordingly.

LACE BONNET

This charming bonnet will frame a baby's face beautifully.
It is an ideal gift for a new baby and the embroidery and
lace design matches that of the Christening gown.

Materials
- *6in (15cm) of 45in (115cm) wide white Swiss batiste or voile*
- *1yd (1m) of ¹/₂in (12mm) wide white Swiss insertion*
- *²/₃yd (60cm) of ³/₈in (1cm) wide white insertion lace*
- *1¹/₄yds (1.2m) of ⁵/₈in (1.5cm) wide white edging lace*
- *1¹/₄yds (1.2m) of ¹/₂in (12mm) wide white double-sided satin ribbon*
- *White embroidery thread*

Size
To fit a baby of 3–6 months

Templates
Crown and back of bonnet, page 119
Single daisy embroidery design, page 121

Skill Level
Easy, 2–3 hours

1 Cut a 5¹/₂ × 17in (14 × 43cm) rectangle of batiste. Cut two 16in (40cm) long strips of Swiss insertion and one of insertion lace. Sew a strip of Swiss insertion to each side of the insertion lace. Try to match the designs of the two Swiss insertion strips.

2 Position the fabric so that the center of one long side of the rectangle aligns with the center of the lace and Swiss insertion band. Sew the fabric to one of the Swiss insertion strips. Trim off the excess fabric from the Swiss insertion strip on the other side of the band.

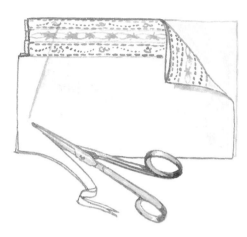

3 Fold the rectangle in half widthwise. Pin it to the crown of bonnet template so that the fold is on the fold line, the lace band along the straight edge of the template and the plain fabric overhangs the curved line. Cut out and gather the fabric edge between the points marked on the template.

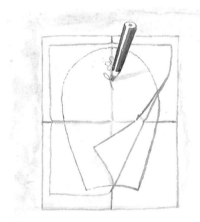

4 Cut a 4 × 5in (10 × 12.5cm) rectangle of fabric. To find the center, fold it in half lengthwise and lightly press. Place the fabric rectangle on the back of bonnet template, lining up the center crease with the center of the template. Trace the single daisy design centrally above the V shape shown on the template. Shape some insertion lace into the V design. Sew the lace V in place, cutting away the fabric from behind it.

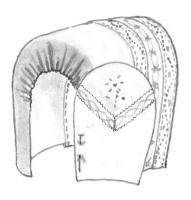

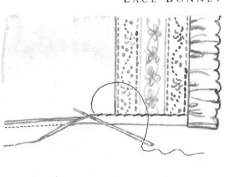

5 Using one strand of white embroidery thread, sew the small daisy above the center of the lace V shape. Pin the embroidered fabric to the back of bonnet template, aligning it correctly, and cut out. Straight stitch this to the gathered edge of the crown of the bonnet, right sides together, using a ³⁄₈in (1cm) seam allowance. Spread the gathers to just below the arms of the V shape. Straight stitch again ⅛in (3mm) outside the first stitching line. Trim back the fabric to this line and press the seam towards the center of the V shape.

6 Cut out a second back of bonnet piece. Stay stitch along the ³⁄₈in (1cm) seam allowance. Trim and clip the seam, turn it under to the wrong side of the fabric, and press along the stay stitching line. Pin the lining piece over the back panel on the inside of the bonnet, wrong sides together, and slip stitch in place.

7 On the crown of the bonnet, sew gathered edging lace to the outer edges of both of the Swiss insertion strips. Leave ½in (12mm) tails of lace at each end of the strip nearest the face opening. Cut a 1 × 10in (2.5 × 25cm) strip of fabric on the straight of grain. Fold in a ¼in (6mm) turning at each end of the strip and straight stitch it to the neck edge of the bonnet, right sides facing and using a ¼in (6mm) seam allowance. Trim the seam, press the binding to the inside of the bonnet and slip stitch in place, turning under the raw edge of the binding as you stitch.

8 Turn under the ends of the outer edging lace and slip stitch in place so that they are in line with the neck binding of the bonnet. Cut the satin ribbon into two equal lengths and sew one to the outer strip of Swiss insertion on each side of the bonnet for ties.

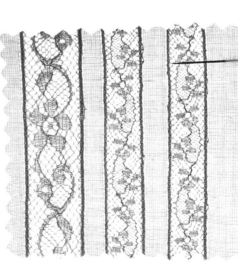

Variations & Tips
• Make a ribbon or lace rosette to stitch on each side of the bonnet where the ribbon ties are attached.
• If you have made the Christening gown, you will have enough fabric left over to make the bonnet.

FRILLY BIB

Practical yet beautiful, this bib can be worn to protect
the bodice of the Christening gown from spills and stains,
but is equally suitable for other special occasions.

Materials

• ¹/₃yd (30cm) of 45in (115cm) wide white Swiss batiste or voile
• ¹/₄yd (25cm) of 45in (115cm) wide white winceyette/flannelette
• ¹/₃yd (30cm) of ¹/₂in (12mm) wide white Swiss insertion
• 1yd (1m) of ¹/₈in (3mm) wide white entredeux
• 1³/₄yds (1.6m) of ⁵/₈in (1.5cm) wide white edging lace
• 4in (10cm) of ¹/₈in (3mm) wide white double-sided satin ribbon
• Small button

Templates

Bib, page 120

Skill Level

Easy, 2–3 hours

1 Cut three bib pieces from Swiss batiste and one from winceyette. To make the back section of the bib, place two of the fabric pieces together, rights sides facing, and then lay them on top of the winceyette piece. Straight stitch all three together around the outside edge and the back opening, using a ¹/₄in (6mm) seam allowance. Do not sew the neck edge at this point. Trim and clip the seam, turn the fabric right side out so that the winceyette is sandwiched between the two batiste pieces, and press.

2 To make the front of the bib, measure 1³/₄in (4.5cm) in from each side edge of the remaining fabric piece and cut it lengthwise on the straight of grain so that it is now in three sections. Cut two 6in (15cm) strips of Swiss insertion. Join the three pieces of fabric back together by sewing the cut edges of the fabric to the strips of Swiss insertion, starting at the bottom edge and matching the lace designs.

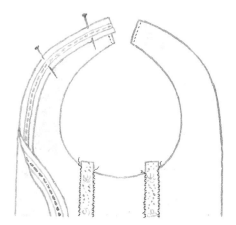

3 Turn under ¹/₈in (3mm) and then ¹/₄in (6mm) of fabric on the back opening edges of the front bib piece and straight stitch in place. Next, sew entredeux all around

the outside edge of the bib front and then sew gathered edging lace to the entredeux, making the gathers fuller at the corners. Leave a ¹/₂in (12mm) tail of lace at each end of the lace and entredeux.

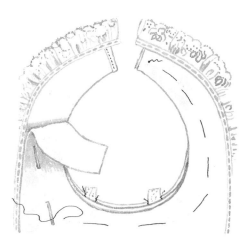

4 Pin the back section of the bib to the wrong side of the bib front. Trim the neck edges to match and baste the two sections together around the neck. Cut a bias strip of batiste measuring ⁷/₈ × 13¹/₂in (2 × 34cm) and use it to bind the neck edge. Sew through all layers of the fabric.

5 Turn under and slip stitch the tails of lace and entredeux at the back opening to neaten. Sew a button to one side of the back opening, and a ribbon loop to the other side.

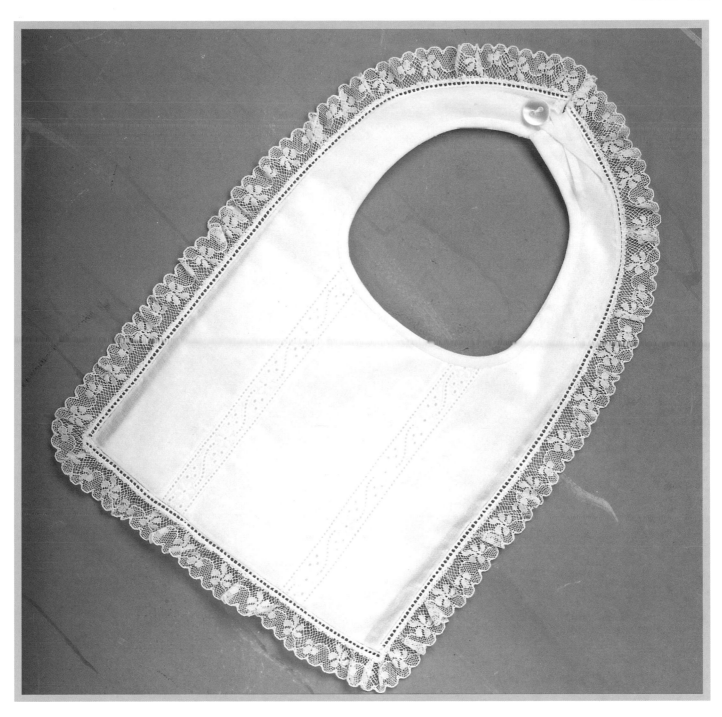

Variations & Tips
● If you are also making the Christening gown, make the bib from left-over pieces of fabric.
● The bib would make a charming gift made in pastel colors with white laces.

BABY BOOTEES

These exquisite lace-decorated bootees complete the Christening ensemble. They are so tiny that everyone will be amazed at the intricacy of your needlework!

Materials

- ¼yd (25cm) of 45in (115cm) wide white Swiss batiste or voile
- ⅓yd (30cm) of ⅜in (1cm) wide white insertion lace
- 1yd (1m) of ⅜in (1cm) wide white edging lace
- 1yd (1m) of ½in (12mm) wide white double-sided satin ribbon
- Heavy-weight interfacing
- Medium-weight interfacing
- White embroidery thread

Size

To fit a baby of 3–6 months

Templates

Upper bootee and sole, page 120
Single daisy embroidery design, page 121

Skill Level

Intermediate, 3–4 hours

1 Cut four upper bootees and four soles in Swiss batiste. Cut two upper bootees in medium-weight interfacing and two soles in heavy-weight interfacing. Cut six 1in (2.5cm) strips of ribbon. Fold each ribbon strip in half to form six ½in (12mm) loops and press. The ribbon ties will be threaded through these loops later.

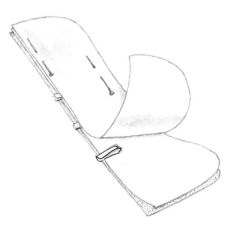

2 Pin the pieces of the upper bootees together, layering them in the following order: interfacing, fabric right-side up, three loops of ribbon positioned as marked on the template (the cut edges of the ribbon will be sewn into the seam allowance), and then a second piece of fabric right-side down. Straight stitch along the straight edges of both bootees using a ¼in (6mm) seam allowance. Trim the seams to ⅛in (3mm), turn the layers right side out so that the interfacing is sandwiched between two pieces of fabric, and press.

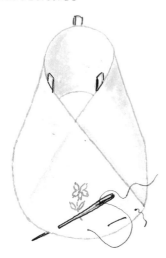

5 Place the interfacing sole pieces between two fabric pieces, both right side out. Straight stitch around the outside edges using a ¹/₈in (3mm) seam allowance and press.

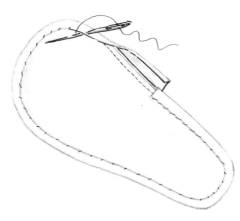

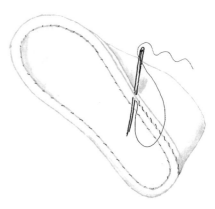

3 Cross over the two curved front sections of each bootee. The top of the cross-over points will be 3in (7.5cm) from the center back ribbon loops. Tack the cross-over points in place. Embroider a small daisy with one strand of thread on the center front of each bootee, i.e. where the front sections overlap, stitching through the top layer of fabric only. Baste around the bottom edge of each bootee to hold all the layers of fabric and interfacing together.

6 Cut four ⁷/₈ × 10in (2 × 25cm) bias strips of fabric. Starting at the instep with a turned-under edge, bind the soles of both bootees using two of the bias strips.

7 Place the upper bootees over the soles and trim to fit if necessary. Pay particular attention to the fit around the curved front section. Bind the bottom edge of the upper bootees with the remaining two bias strips, again starting at the instep. Pin the upper bootees to the soles, matching the center fronts and center backs, and whip the bound edges together on the outside.

8 Whip stitch gathered edging lace around the top edge and down the outside edges of the insertion lace on the front of the upper bootees. Thread ribbon through the loops and tie at the front.

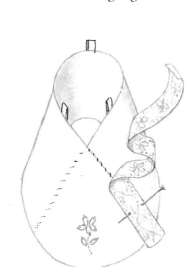

4 Secure the overlapped fabric on both the inside and outside of the bootees by slip stitching the fabric in place. Pin the insertion lace so that it lies with the center of the lace over the slip-stitched joins. Miter the lace at the upper edge of each bootee and zigzag the miters in place.

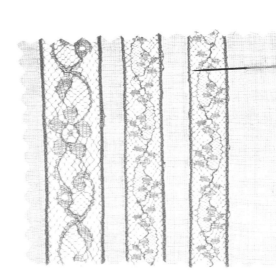

Variations & Tips
- Sew the ribbon loops by hand using buttonhole stitch.
- A simpler variation could be made in a pastel color without the edging lace or hand embroidery.

SWEETHEART QUILT

Pastel-colored lacy hearts are the perfect design for a baby's quilt and are really very simple to do. A smaller version of this quilt would be perfect for a child's doll.

Materials
- 2½yds (2.3m) of 45in (115cm) wide white cotton fabric
- Two 9in (23cm) squares of cotton fabric in each of the following pastel colors: blue, pink, turquoise and peach
- 4¼yds (4m) of ½in (12mm) wide white insertion lace
- 5½yds (5.3m) of 2in (5cm) wide white edging lace
- Batting
- Fusible web (optional)

Templates
Large and small hearts, page 118

Skill Level
Intermediate, 12–14 hours

1 Find the center point of each of the pastel squares by folding them in half lengthwise and widthwise and pressing lightly along these folds. Using the template as a guide, shape the insertion lace into a large heart on the center of one of the blue squares. Shape a small lace heart onto the other blue square.

2 Repeat this for the remaining six squares so that you have four different-colored squares with large hearts and four different-colored squares with small hearts. Sew the lace in place and cut away the fabric from the outer edges of the heart shapes only. Do not cut away the fabric from behind the lace.

3 Cut a 23 × 28in (58 × 71cm) rectangle of white cotton fabric. Fold it in half lengthwise and widthwise, and press along the folds so that the point where they intersect is the exact center of the fabric. Position the large lace hearts around the center of the fabric so that the top and bottom points of each heart lie along one of the four fold lines. The bottom points of the hearts should be positioned 1in (2.5cm) away from the center of the fabric. Pin them in place.

4 Choose a regular color arrangement and position one of the small hearts at each corner of the fabric, all pointing downward. Each heart should be placed 2in (5cm) in from the edges. Pin them in place. Use a small zigzag to stitch the outside edge of the hearts in place. Press to remove any creases. The hearts can be fused in place with fusible web, if preferred.

5 Using the ½in (12mm) seam allowance as a guide, straight stitch the gathered edging lace around the quilt front. Make the gathers fuller at three of the corners and miter the lace at the fourth. Zigzag the mitered corner and trim off any excess lace.

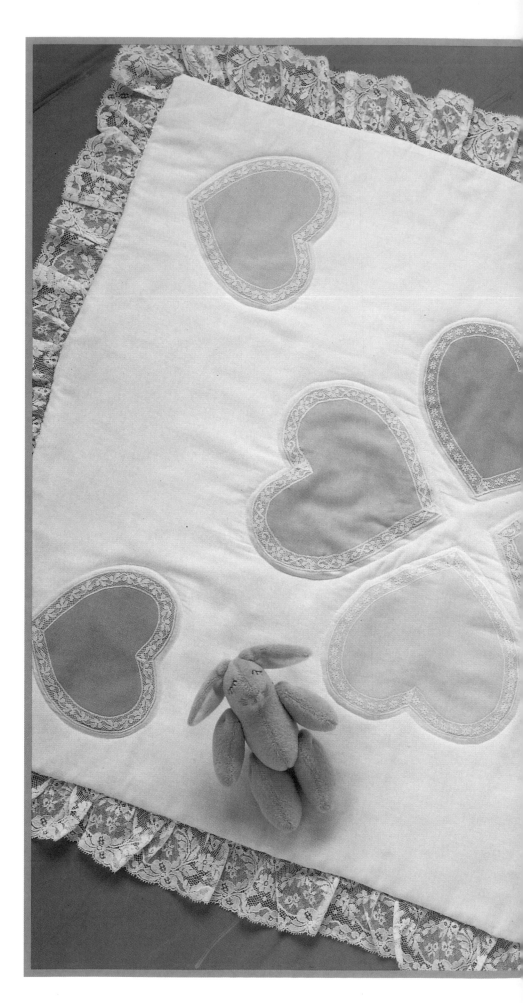

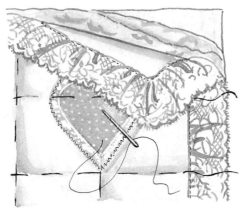

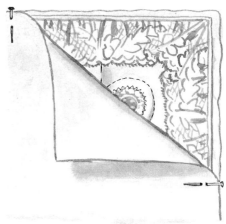

6 Cut two rectangles of white cotton fabric and one of batting. They should all be 1in (2.5cm) bigger than the quilt front, i.e. 24 × 29in (61 × 74cm). Place the layer of batting on one of the rectangles of fabric and then lay the quilt front, face upward, on top. Tack all three layers together, spacing the tacking rows about 2in (5cm) apart. This will prevent the layers from slipping while quilting around the hearts. Starting with the center hearts first, quilt around each one using a long straight stitch sewn just outside of the lace.

7 Straight stitch the three layers together around the outside edge following the stitching line for the edging lace. Lay the second rectangle of fabric on top of the quilt front, right sides facing. Make sure that the edging lace lies inward toward the center of the quilt so that it is sandwiched between the cotton and the quilt front. Pin the cotton in place and then turn the whole thing over so that the quilt front faces down. Straight stitch around the outside edge of the quilt following the previous stitching lines and leaving a 6in (15cm) opening.

8 Turn the quilt right side out to check if any of the edging lace has been caught in the stitching. Unpick and restitch if necessary. Turn the quilt to the wrong side again, trim off any excess fabric and batting, and overlock the edges with a zigzag stitch. Turn the quilt right side out and stitch the opening closed.

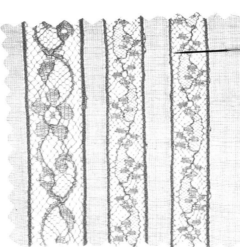

Variations & Tips
• Use strong primary colors for the hearts and sew contrasting piping around the edges of the quilt.
• Substitute gingham for the white cotton with hearts in matching pastel colors.
• Embroider decorative designs inside each of the hearts.

WOOLEN SHAWL

*This luxurious lace-trimmed shawl is surprisingly easy
to make. Wrapped up snugly, the baby will feel comforted
and protected whatever the weather.*

Materials

- *57in (144cm) square of ivory wool challis/vyella*
- *6¹/₂yds (6m) of 1in (2.5cm) wide ivory insertion lace*
- *7yds (6.5m) of 2in (5cm) wide ivory edging lace*

Skill Level

Easy, 4–5 hours

1 Cut the ivory wool fabric into three strips, each measuring 19 × 57in (48 × 144cm). Sew a 57in (144cm) strip of ivory insertion lace down both long edges of one of the fabric strips. This will form the central panel of the shawl.

2 Take the remaining two fabric strips, fold them in half lengthwise along the straight of grain, and press. Sew one to each side of the central panel of the shawl along the insertion laces. When sewing the fabric to the lace, take care to keep the top and bottom edges of the shawl level. You may need to pull the fabric toward you to keep the bottom edges even.

3 Cut the two outer fabric rectangles along the fold lines and then join them back together with two more 57in (144cm) strips of insertion lace.

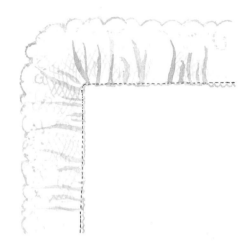

4 Roll and whip all four edges of the shawl, then attach the edging lace. Start at a corner, leaving a 2¹/₂in (6cm) tail of lace. Loosely gather the lace for 4in (10cm), then straight stitch to within 4in (10cm) from the next corner and loosely gather the lace up to the corner. Repeat until you return to the first corner. Miter the lace at this corner and then zigzag the miter in place.

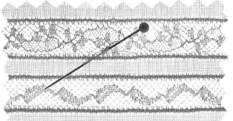

Variations & Tips

- Alter the position of the insertion laces according to taste. For example, you may wish to have two strips of lace closer together along each side.
- The baby's initials can be embroidered on a corner of the shawl.

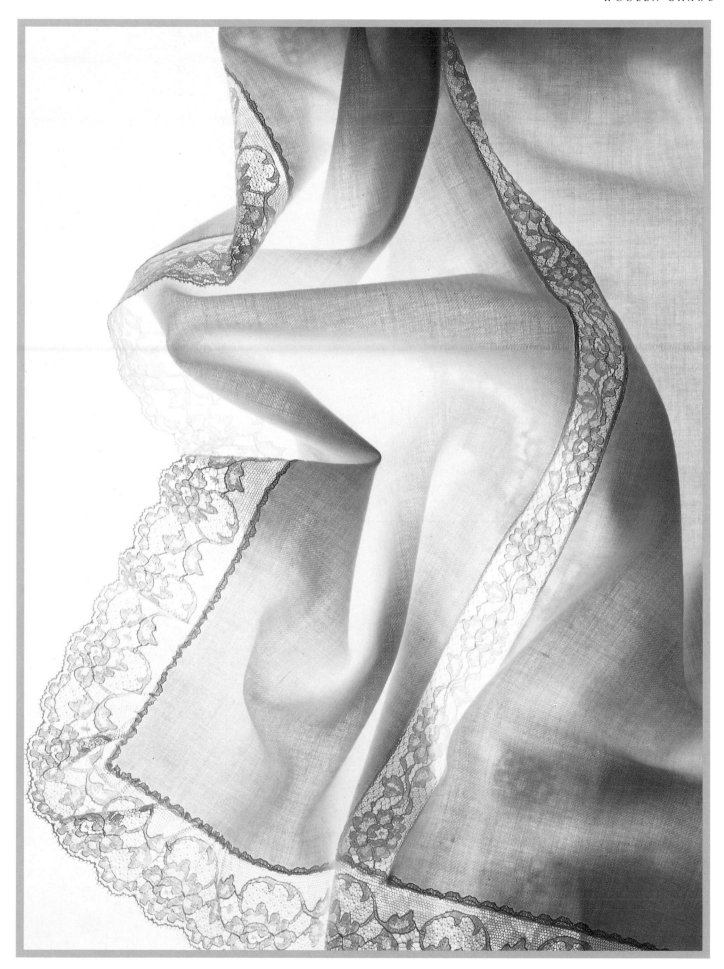

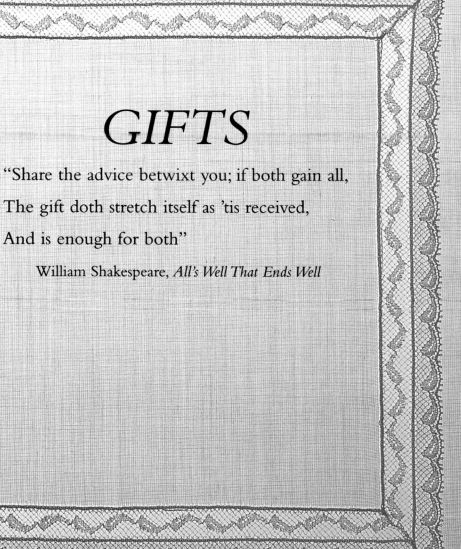

GIFTS

"Share the advice betwixt you; if both gain all,
The gift doth stretch itself as 'tis received,
And is enough for both"

William Shakespeare, *All's Well That Ends Well*

COAT HANGERS

The ultimate luxury for your wardrobe, these padded coat hangers are a perfect gift by themselves, or with a potpourri sachet to keep clothes wrinkle-free and subtly perfumed.

NET LACE COAT HANGER

Materials
- ¼yd (25cm) of 45in (115cm) wide peach silk satin
- ½yd (50cm) of 45in (115cm) wide black net
- ½yd (50cm) of 2in (5cm) wide black net edging lace
- 5 black guipure lace motifs
- 17in (43cm) long wooden coat hanger
- Batting

Templates
Satin and net covers, page 122

Skill Level
Easy, 3–4 hours

EMBROIDERED COAT HANGER

Materials
- ¼yd (25cm) of 45in (115cm) wide white cotton fabric
- Small pieces of floral print fabric and matching plain fabric (yellow is used here)
- ¾yd (70cm) of floral print piping
- 1¼yds (1.2m) of ½in (12mm) wide white insertion lace
- 1yd (1m) of 1½in (4cm) wide white edging lace
- Small piece of 1in (2.5cm) wide white edging lace
- 1yd (1m) of ⅛in (3mm) wide white entredeux
- Medium-weight interfacing
- 17in (43cm) long wooden coat hanger
- Batting
- Embroidery threads in the following colors: DMC 503 (green), 744 (mid yellow), 745 (pale yellow)

Templates
Embroidered cover, page 122
Bow and roses embroidery design, page 121

Skill Level
Intermediate, 4–5 hours

NET LACE COAT HANGER

1 Cut out two coat hanger pieces in peach silk satin and two in black net. Cut a 1 × 8in (2.5 × 20cm) bias strip of peach satin. Fold the bias strip in half lengthwise, right sides together. Sew across one end and about halfway along its length, ¼in (6mm) in from the fold. You need to sew a long enough section to fit over the hook of the coat hanger. Trim back the seam allowance and turn right side out. Slip the strip over the hook.

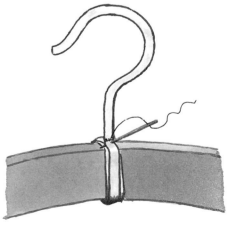

2 Stretch the strip along the hook and wind the remainder around the coat hanger. Slip stitch the strip firmly in place at the base of the hook so that the fabric cover does not work loose. Wind 2in (5cm) wide strips of batting around the coat hanger, stitching it in place at each end.

3 With right sides facing and using a ½in (12mm) seam allowance, sew the two peach satin pieces together from the center top, down to one end of the hanger, and all along the bottom edge. Do not sew the remaining half of the top edge. Trim and clip the seams, turn the cover right side out and press. Slip it over the batting of the coat hanger and stitch the remaining top edge closed by hand.

EMBROIDERED COAT HANGER

1 Follow the instructions in Steps 1 and 2 for the Net Lace Coat Hanger to cover the hook with floral print fabric and the wooden hanger with batting.

2 Embroider the green bow, and the yellow and green roses design onto a piece of white fabric. Cut the fabric down to 5 × 4½in (12.5 × 11.5cm) with the center of the bow positioned 1¼in (3cm) below one of the longer edges (this will be the top of the panel). Sew entredeux to both sides of the panel. Cut two 5 × 4½in (12.5 × 11.5cm) rectangles of white fabric.

3 Cut five 9in (23cm) strips of insertion lace and sew them together lengthwise. Cut the finished lace panel in half. Cut two 3 × 4½in (7.5 × 11.5cm) rectangles of plain colored fabric. Straight stitch the lace panels onto the colored fabric along both long edges, leaving a ¼in

4 Using a ¼in (6mm) seam allowance straight stitch the two net pieces together along the top edge and sides only, leaving a small opening for the hook. Slip the net over the hanger and position the lace motifs attractively along its length. Pin them to the net only and then remove the net cover and straight stitch the motifs in place. Trim back the seams on the net and replace it over the hanger.

5 Along the bottom edge and as close to the coat hanger as possible, straight stitch the edging lace to the front piece of the net, leaving a tail of lace at each end. Zigzag the tails under and trim. Straight stitch the back of the net cover to the front, following the stitching line for the edging lace. Sew a second row of stitching ⅛in (3mm) below the first. Trim off any excess net at the back of the cover.

(6mm) seam allowance at each side. Straight stitch down both edges of the central strip of insertion lace to hold the lace panel firmly in place.

4 Sew a strip of entredeux to each side of the lace panels. Sew a lace panel to either side of the embroidered fabric through the entredeux. Sew a rectangle of white fabric to the entredeux on the other side of each lace panel.

5 Pin the finished rectangle over the embroidered cover template, ensuring that the center of the bow is on the fold line and 1¼in (3cm) from the top edge. Cut out the front cover. Thread 4 strands of green embroidery thread through each strip of entredeux.

6 Cut three more pattern pieces in white fabric and two in interfacing. For the front section of the cover, lay a piece of interfacing on the wrong side of the embroidered piece and then one of the white fabric pieces. Tack the top edge and sides together. Tack the back section of the cover in the same way with the remaining piece of interfacing between the last two white fabric pieces.

7 Using a ¼in (6mm) seam allowance, sew the piping along the sides and top edge of the front section, raw edges even. With right

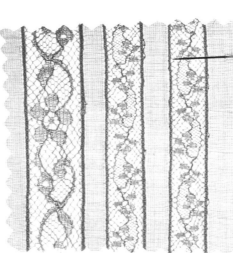

sides facing and following the stitching line for the piping, sew the front and back sections together, leaving a gap for the hook. Trim and clip the seam. Turn right side out.

8 Turn under a ¼in (6mm) seam allowance on both the front and back sections of the cover, and press. Cut an 18in (45cm) strip of entredeux and sew gathered 1½in (4cm) wide edging lace to it. Sew the entredeux to the embroidered front piece only along the folded line. Turn under and zigzag each end of the lace to neaten.

9 Place the cover on the hanger. Gather 1in (2.5cm) wide edging lace into a circle, slip it over the hook and stitch it in place, closing any gap at the same time. Slip stitch the back of the cover to the front along the top edge of the entredeux and the folded line.

Variations & Tips

• Decorate the base of the hook on the net lace hanger with bows of black or peach satin ribbon.
• The embroidered coat hanger would be perfect for hanging a wedding gown.

POTPOURRI SACHETS

*Keep your lingerie and clothes lightly perfumed with these
lace sachets. Quick and easy to make, they are a charming
gift for birthdays or to fill a Christmas stocking.*

CIRCULAR AND RECTANGULAR SACHETS

Materials
• *Small pieces of peach and turquoise silk satin*
• *Small pieces of black and cream net*
• *¾yd (70cm) each of black and cream edging lace – any width will do*
• *1 black and 1 cream guipure lace motifs*
• *Potpourri*

Skill Level
Easy, 1–2 hours

EMBROIDERED SACHET

Materials
• *Small pieces of white and floral fabric*
• *½yd (50cm) of ⅝in (1.5cm) wide white insertion lace*
• *¾yd (70cm) of ⅝in (1.5cm) wide white edging lace*
• *½yd (50cm) of ⅛in (3mm) wide white entredeux*
• *Embroidery threads in the following colors: DMC 503 (green), 744 (mid yellow), 745 (pale yellow)*
• *Potpourri*

Templates
Roses embroidery design, page 121

Skill Level
Intermediate, 4–5 hours

CIRCULAR SACHET

1 Cut out two circles of peach satin, each with a diameter of 5in (12.5cm). With right sides facing, stitch the two pieces together, leaving an opening of 2in (5cm). Trim and clip the seam. Turn right side out, press and fill the sachet with potpourri. Slip stitch the opening closed.

2 Encase the sachet with black net and position a black guipure lace motif on top so that it sits in the center of the sachet. Pin the motif to the net, then remove the net from the sachet and straight stitch the motif in place.

3 Replace the stitched motif and net around the sachet so that the sachet is completely encased and the lace motif is correctly centered. Pin the net around the sachet and, using a small zigzag, sew the black edging lace to the net following the shape of the sachet. Gently gather the edging lace around the entire circumference of the circle. Cut away any excess net from behind the edging lace as close to the zigzag stitching as possible.

RECTANGULAR SACHET

1 Cut out two 6 × 4in (15 × 10cm) rectangles of turquoise satin. Sew them together in the same way as the circular sachet and fill with potpourri. Decorate it with cream net and lace. When attaching the edging lace, gather it around the corners only.

EMBROIDERED SACHET

1 Embroider the yellow and green roses design onto a piece of white fabric large enough to fit into an embroidery hoop. When the embroidery is finished, cut the fabric into a rectangle measuring 2½ × 3½in (6 × 9cm). Make sure that the embroidery sits in the center of the rectangle. Sew entredeux around each side of the embroidered rectangle.

2 Sew insertion lace to the entredeux around all four sides of the rectangle, mitering the lace at each corner. Thread 4 strands of green embroidery thread through the entredeux, threading it back on itself to secure the ends.

3 Cut a 3½ × 4½in (9 × 11.5cm) rectangle of floral fabric and roll and whip all four sides. Stitch gathered edging lace around the fabric, gathering it more fully at three of the corners and mitering the fourth. Pin the floral fabric and embroidered panel together, right sides facing. Make sure that the gathered lace is facing inward toward the center of the floral rectangle. Straight stitch together following the line of stitching for the gathered lace and leaving a 2in (5cm) opening. Turn the sachet right side out. Fill with potpourri and stitch the opening closed.

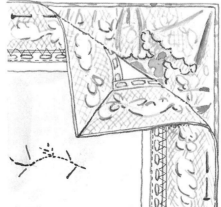

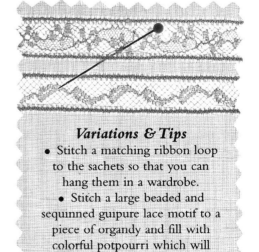

Variations & Tips

• Stitch a matching ribbon loop to the sachets so that you can hang them in a wardrobe.

• Stitch a large beaded and sequinned guipure lace motif to a piece of organdy and fill with colorful potpourri which will show through the lace.

PICTURE FRAMES

Precious memories deserve to be framed in beautiful laces.
Match the colors to the decor of the room where the
photographs will be displayed.

BEADED FRAME

Materials
• *Green padded rectangular picture frame or "make-your-own" kit – the frame used here measures 9 × 7½in (23 × 19cm) with a 5 × 3½in (12.5 × 9cm) aperture*
• *11 × 9½in (28 × 24cm) scrap of green chintz (if using a kit)*
• *1yd (1m) of 1½in (4cm) wide ivory net edging lace*
• *1¼yds (1.2m) of small pearl beading-by-the-yard*
• *½yd (50cm) of ⅛in (3mm) wide cream silk ribbon*
• *Fabric glue or hot glue gun (if using a kit)*

Skill Level
Easy, 3 hours

DAISY FRAME

Materials
• *Pale blue padded oval picture frame with detachable back or "make-your-own" kit – the frame used here measures 9 × 7in (23 × 18cm) with a 6 × 4in (15 × 10cm) aperture*
• *⅓yd (30cm) of 45in (115cm) wide pale blue cotton fabric (if using a kit)*
• *3½in (9cm) of 45in (115cm) wide pale blue cotton fabric (if using a ready-made frame)*
• *1yd (1m) of ½in (12mm) wide white Swiss insertion*

• *2yds (1.8m) of 1in (2.5cm) wide white edging lace*
• *1yd (1m) of ¼in (6mm) wide pale blue silk ribbon*
• *¼yd (25cm) of ⅛in (3mm) wide pale blue silk ribbon*
• *White embroidery thread*
• *Fabric glue or hot glue gun*

Skill Level
Intermediate, 4 hours

ANTIQUE FRAME

Materials
• *Royal blue padded picture frame with a detachable back or "make-your-own" kit – the frame used here measures 7 × 5in (18 × 13cm)*
• *9 × 7in (23 × 18cm) scrap of royal blue chintz (if using a kit)*
• *Assortment of antique laces (tiny scraps will do)*
• *Selection of charms, beads and lace rosettes*
• *Fabric glue or hot glue gun*

Skill Level
Easy, 1–2 hours

BEADED FRAME

1 Assemble the picture frame. If using a ready-made frame, it does not matter if the front and back are fused together.

2 Pin the net edging lace around the front of the frame so that the decorative edge of the lace is even with the outside edge of the frame. Trim off any excess lace from the inside edge if necessary (an inner rectangle of fabric should remain visible). Miter the corners of the lace and remove it from the frame. Stitch the miters in place, trim off any excess lace and press. Reposition the lace on the frame and slip stitch it in place along the inside edge. Catch the outer corners and edges of the lace to the frame where necessary to ensure a tight fit.

3 Whip stitch the pearl beading around the central aperture of the frame and the inside edge of the lace. Attach a small ribbon bow at each corner, positioned on the inside edge of the lace.

ANTIQUE FRAME

1 Make lace rosettes by running a line of gathering stitches along one long edge of a strip of lace. Draw it up tightly to form a rosette and secure with a few back stitches.

DAISY FRAME

1 If using a kit, assemble the picture frame but do not fuse the back of the frame to the front.

2 If using a kit, assemble the picture frame but do not fuse the back of the frame to the front. Arrange the antique laces, beads and rosettes attractively on the front of the frame and either stitch or glue them in place, allowing the tails of lace to fold to the back of the frame. Fuse the back of the frame in place, securing the lace tails at the same time.

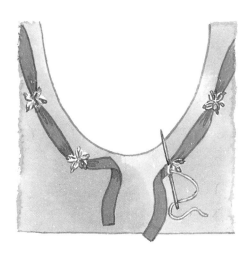

2 Whip stitch Swiss insertion around the outside edge of the front of the frame, mitering the corners. Sew ¼in (6mm) wide silk ribbon around the oval aperture using one strand of embroidery thread and lazy daisy stitch to catch it down at regular intervals. At the bottom of the ribbon oval, stitch a bow made from ⅛in (3mm) wide silk ribbon to disguise the join.

3 Cut a 3½ × 45in (9 × 115cm) strip of blue fabric and sew the short ends together, right sides facing. Press the seam open, then fold the strip in half lengthwise, wrong sides facing, and press. Sew two gathering rows along the raw edges of the strip to allow it to be gathered at the corners of the frame.

4 Gather the edging lace so that it fits around the frame and join the two ends. Whip stitch the lace and fabric frill together, taking care that the decorative outer edges are even. Glue the fabric side of the completed frill to the back of the frame as close to the edge as possible. Assemble the frame and glue a loop of ribbon to the back so that it can be hung on the wall.

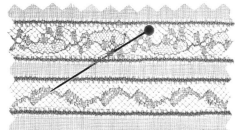

Variations & Tips
- Seal any clipped edges of lace around the picture frame apertures with Fray Check.
- Omit the frill from the daisy frame if you would prefer it to be free-standing – the daisy design and Swiss insertion border are very pretty on their own.

PINCUSHIONS

Any friend who sews will appreciate the delicacy and practicality of these pincushions. Or why not make one for your own sewing room? They make an ideal first project.

VELVET PINCUSHION

Materials
- *6in (15cm) diameter circle of red velvet*
- *Three motifs from cream guipure edging lace*
- *Small round beads in coordinating colors*
- *4in (10cm) diameter Victorian reproduction wooden pin holder base and pincushion pad*
- *Quilting thread*

Skill Level
Easy, 3 hours

LOG CABIN PINCUSHION

Materials
- *Two 6in (15cm) squares of lilac upholstery velvet*
- *¾yd (70cm) each of ⅝in (1.5cm) wide cream insertion lace in two different designs*
- *¾yd (70cm) of 1½in (4cm) wide cream guipure edging lace*
- *2in (5cm) square cream lace motif*
- *Batting*

Templates
Log cabin square, page 123

Skill Level
Easy, 2–3 hours

VELVET PINCUSHION

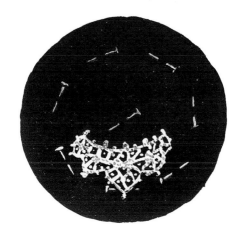

1 Mark the center of the velvet circle with a pin and then lay the pincushion pad on the velvet, centers aligned. Mark the circumference of the base of the pincushion pad on the velvet with pins.

2 Remove the pad and place three guipure lace motifs in a circle around the center pin and just inside the marked circumference line (the decorative edging may overlap slightly). When you are satisfied with the arrangement, straight stitch the motifs in place and then remove the pins. Decorate the motifs with beads.

3 Using quilting thread, sew a row of running stitches around the velvet circle, ¼in (6mm) in from the raw edge. Place the velvet over the pincushion pad, ensuring that the center of the velvet circle is aligned with the center of the pad.

4 Draw up the running thread and secure with back stitches. Sew a few herringbone stitches across the back of the pincushion pad, catching in the gathers to hold the velvet taut and firm. Assemble the velvet and lace covered pad with the wooden base, making sure that the excess velvet is held neatly between the pad and the wooden base.

LOG CABIN PINCUSHION

1 Sew strips of insertion lace around the lace motif in a log cabin design. Follow the alphabetical order shown on the template, alternating two strips of one lace design with two strips of the other design. Cut each strip of lace 1in (2.5cm) longer than shown on the

template to allow overlaps at the corners. Trim off any excess lace behind each zigzagged seam once the next strip has been attached.

2 Lay the finished lace patchwork square on top of one of the squares of velvet. Make sure that the edges of the lace patchwork form a true square and that it is centrally positioned on the velvet. Pin it in place and zigzag the edges of the lace to the velvet. There should be ½in (12mm) of velvet visible all around the lace patchwork square.

3 Take the second piece of velvet and place it on top of the first, right sides facing. Stitch around all four sides just outside of the line of zigzag stitching. Leave a 2in (5cm) opening. Trim and clip the corners of the seams. Turn right side out and fill the pin cushion with batting. Stitch the opening closed.

4 Whip stitch guipure edging lace all around the patchwork square. Arrange the edging lace so that you reach the end of an individual motif right at the corner point of the square. Fold the next motif to the front and start stitching at the beginning of the following motif, sewing it to the same corner point. Continue stitching the lace along the sides, repeating this process at each corner. Press the corner motifs flat and slip stitch the center of each one to the corners to hold in place.

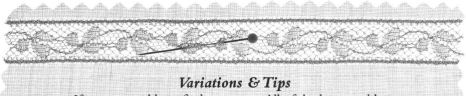

Variations & Tips

• If you are unable to find a suitable lace motif for the center of the log cabin patchwork square, use an attractive scrap of fabric instead of lace.

• All of the laces used here are antique. These pincushions are an ideal way to use some of the smaller pieces from your antique lace collection.

SEWING ROLL

This is the sewing kit of your dreams. It is the perfect way to keep your embroidery threads in complementary color groups, with large pockets for accessories and patterns.

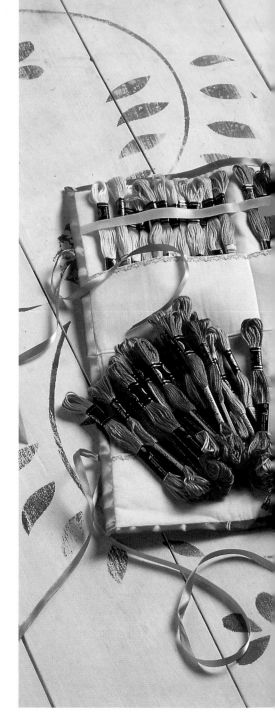

Materials

- ½yd (50cm) of 45in (115cm) wide floral fabric
- 1yd (1m) of 45in (115cm) wide cream cotton fabric
- 2¼yds (2.1m) of ½in (12mm) wide satin ribbon, either cream to match the inside of the roll or colored to coordinate with the floral fabric
- 3½yds (3.2m) of ½in (12mm) wide satin ribbon to coordinate with the floral fabric
- 2yds (1.8m) of ¼in (6mm) wide satin ribbon to coordinate with the floral fabric
- 16in (40cm) strip of 1⅛in (3cm) wide plain white Swiss insertion, suitable for embroidery
- 4yds (3.7m) of ½in (12mm) wide white Swiss insertion
- ½yd (50cm) of ½in (12mm) wide white Swiss edging
- Heavy-weight interfacing
- 12in (30cm) white Velcro strip
- Embroidery threads in the following colors: DMC 223 (dark pink), 3354 (medium pink), 340 (dark mauve), 211 (lilac), 292 (yellow), 3817 (green)

Templates

Floral trail embroidery design, page 121

Skill Level

Advanced, 8–10 hours

1 Embroider the floral trail design onto the 16in (40cm) strip of plain Swiss insertion. Sew a strip of ½in (12mm) wide Swiss insertion to each side of the embroidered strip and then sew Swiss edging to one side of this. Trim back the fabric edge on the other side of this band to ¼in (6mm). All of the Swiss laces used here are edged with entredeux so simply zigzag between the holes when stitching them together.

2 Cut a 16 × 42in (40 × 107cm) rectangle of floral fabric. Cut a rectangle of cream cotton fabric and a rectangle of heavy-weight interfacing to the same size. Fuse the interfacing to the wrong side of the floral fabric.

3 Pin the lace band along one of the short sides of the floral fabric, keeping the raw edge of the Swiss insertion even with the fabric edge. Sew the lace band to the floral fabric by first stitching in the ditch along the fabric edge of the lace band, and then along the entredeux seam on the inner edge.

4 Stitch ½in (12mm) wide Swiss insertion around the remaining three sides of the floral fabric. Trim off the fabric edge from one side of the insertion and trim the other fabric edge back to ¼in (6mm). Starting at the embroidered band, pin the Swiss insertion in place, keeping the fabric edge of the insertion even with the raw edge of the floral fabric. Sew the Swiss insertion to the floral fabric by first straight stitching in the ditch around the outer fabric edge, then zigzagging the inner edge. Miter the corners, including where these strips of lace meet the embroidered band.

5 The sewing roll has two long parallel rows of pockets to hold threads plus two deep pockets on the right to hold accessories. To make the two long rows of pockets, cut two 7 × 36in (18 × 91cm) rectangles of cream fabric and two 3½ × 36in (9 × 91cm) rectangles of interfacing. Fuse a rectangle of interfacing to one half of each of the cream rectangles. Fold the fabric rectangles in half lengthwise with right sides facing. Straight stitch one of the short sides together on each rectangle using a ¼in (6mm) seam allowance. Clip the corners, turn right side out and press.

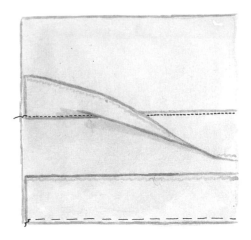

6 Stitch the folded edge of both rectangles with decorative machine embroidery. Place the lower row of pockets onto the large cream rectangle, all raw edges even and square. Pin and baste in place. Position the top row of pockets so that the side raw edge is at the side of the cream rectangle and the long raw edge runs along the center of the rectangle. The embroidered edge should be face down and pointing toward the bottom row of pockets. Straight stitch in place. Flip the top row of pockets upward, press, and edge stitch along the seam to hold in place.

7 To make the two deep pockets, cut two 6 × 13in (15 × 33cm) rectangles of cream fabric and two 6 × 6½in (15 × 16.5cm) rectangles of interfacing. Fuse a rectangle of interfacing to one half of each cream rectangle. Fold the fabric rectangles in half widthwise with right sides facing and raw edges even. Straight stitch one of the sides together on each rectangle using a ¼in (6mm) seam allowance. Clip the corners, turn right side out and press.

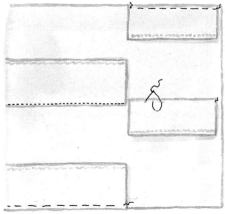

8 To make the two pocket flaps, cut two 6 × 4½in (15 × 11.5cm) rectangles of cream cotton and two 6 × 2¼in (15 × 5.7cm) rectangles of interfacing. Fuse the interfacing to one half of each cream rectangle. Fold the fabric rectangles in half lengthwise, and with right sides facing, straight stitch both short sides together. Clip the corners, turn right side out and press. Decorate the folded edges of the flaps with machine embroidery. Pin and baste one flap to the top edge of the cotton, raw edges even. To position the bottom flap, line up the ¼in (6mm) seam allowance of the raw edge of the flap with the bottom edge of the upper row of pockets. Baste in place.

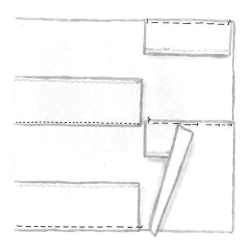

9 Using a ¼in (6mm) seam allowance, pin the bottom raw edge of one of the pockets to the seam allowance of the bottom flap, embroidery face down and side raw edge even with the side raw edge of the large rectangle. The seam

allowances of both the bottom flap and the upper pocket should be level with the line of edge stitching of the upper row of pockets. Straight stitch though all layers. Flip the pocket upwards, press, and edge stitch along the seam to hold it in place.

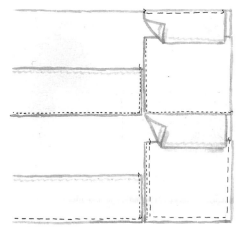

10 Position the lower pocket on the large cream rectangle with side and bottom raw edges even. Baste all three sides. Edge stitch the inside edges of both large pockets and the two long rows of pockets where they meet. Baste the cream and floral rectangles together, wrong sides facing. The embroidered lace band should be positioned at the side with the two long rows of pockets.

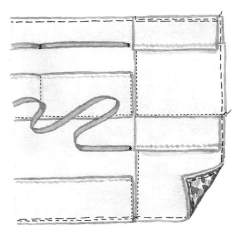

11 Cut the ½in (12mm) wide cream or colored ribbon in half. Place each piece 2in (5cm) above a long row of pockets, turning under the raw end next to the large pockets and zigzagging it in place through all layers. At approximately

6in (15cm) intervals, zigzag the ribbon through all layers, then straight stitch the two rows of pockets through all layers at exactly the same intervals, thus forming the smaller pockets to separate the colors of thread. Stitch strips of Velcro to the pocket flaps and pockets to keep them closed.

12 Bind the raw edges of the sewing roll with ½in (12mm) wide colored ribbon, zigzagging it to the entredeux border and mitering the corners. Take care not to catch the pocket flaps in the stitching.

13 To make the ribbon ties, cut the ¼in (6mm) wide ribbon in half and position each half 3½in (9cm) in from the sides of the lace band. Slip stitch each piece to the ribbon binding so that 12in (30cm) extends beyond the edge of the sewing roll and 24in (61cm) lies across the lace band and along the floral fabric. Roll up the sewing roll along the folds formed by the stitching for the 6in (15cm) pockets. Tie the ribbon into two bows.

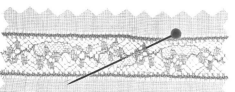

Variations & Tips

- Choose off-white or cream for the inside fabric because these colors do not distort the true color of your threads. White and other colors do not make as good a background.
- Substitute machine embroidery for the hand embroidery on the decorative Swiss lace band.
- Replace the Swiss embroideries with insertion and edging laces.

BEDROOM PILLOW

What a charming addition to a pretty bedroom setting this pillow makes. Use the softest fabrics and laces available, and you will find that it really is as comfortable as it looks.

Materials

- *10in (25cm) long bolster with a 17in (43cm) circumference*
- *½yd (50cm) of 45in (115cm) wide dusky rose cotton sateen*
- *Scrap of cream satin*
- *2yds (1.8m) of 1in (2.5cm) wide off-white net insertion lace*
- *1yd (1m) of ¾in (2cm) wide off-white net beading lace*
- *1yd (1m) of 3in (7.5cm) wide off-white net edging lace*
- *1yd (1m) of ¾in (2cm) wide off-white double-sided satin ribbon*
- *1yd (1m) of ¼in (6mm) wide off-white satin ribbon*
- *1in (2.5cm) self-covering button*

Skill Level

Easy, 3–4 hours

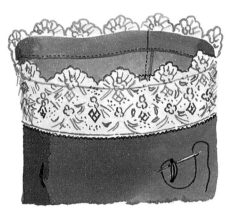

1 From cotton sateen, cut one 18in (46cm) square and one circle with a 6in (15cm) diameter for the base. Cut four 18in (46cm) strips of insertion lace and two strips of beading to the same length.

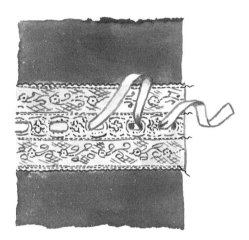

2 Straight stitch a strip of insertion lace onto the square of fabric, positioning it 1½in (4cm) in from one raw edge. Follow this with a strip of beading and then another strip of insertion lace. Repeat this process for the second band of laces, leaving 3in (7.5cm) between the two bands. Thread ¼in (6mm) wide satin ribbon through the beading strips.

3 Fold the square in half, right sides together and matching up the lace bands. Sew into a tube using a ½in (12mm) seam allowance. Trim back the seam to ¼in (6mm) and press to one side. At the end farthest away from the lace bands, turn under and press a ¼in (6mm) seam, then turn under and press a further 1in (2.5cm) hem. Straight stitch in place.

4 Cut the length of edging lace in half and join the raw edges of both pieces to make two circles the same size. Place one of the lace circles around the hemmed end of the fabric tube, positioning it so that 1in (2.5cm) of the decorative edge of the lace protrudes beyond the fabric. Pin and zigzag the straight edge of the lace in place. Next, stitch four ½in (12mm) loops evenly around the fabric circle 1in (2.5cm) below the stitching of the edging lace. These loops will hold the ribbon tie in place.

5 Turn the tube wrong side out and gather the raw edge at its base. Pin, baste and straight stitch the fabric circle to it using a ½in (12mm) seam allowance. Straight stitch a second line of stitching close to the first. Trim the seam to ¼in (6mm), clip close to the stitching, and turn right side out.

6 Sew a running stitch around the straight edge of the remaining lace circle and draw up the thread to make a tightly gathered flat circle. Secure with back stitches. Pin the lace to the pillow base and tack the scalloped edge to the circumference at intervals. The lace will extend approximately $\frac{1}{2}$in (12mm) beyond the base circumference, thereby disguising the seam.

7 Cover the button with cream satin fabric and stitch it over the center of the base. Place the bolster inside the pillow cover. Thread $\frac{3}{4}$in (2cm) wide ribbon through the thread loops, draw it up and tie with a large bow.

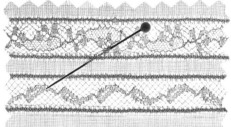

Variations & Tips
- Sew narrow edging lace to a circle of all-over lace for the base if you do not have sufficient wide edging lace.
- Cover the button with lace or ribbon if preferred.

EVENING PURSE

Lace can look splendidly dramatic when combined with sequins and satin. Choose coordinating colors and fabrics to accessorize your favorite evening dress.

Materials

- *½yd (50cm) of 45in (115cm) wide black satin*
- *3¾yds (3.4m) of ⅝in (1.5cm) wide off-white insertion lace*
- *3¼yds (3m) of ⅝in (1.5cm) wide gold sequinned braid*
- *1½yds (1.4m) of ⅝in (1.5cm) wide black satin ribbon*
- *Heavy-weight interfacing*
- *25in (64cm) black Velcro strip*

Skill Level

Intermediate, 5 hours

1 Cut two 12½ × 10½in (32 × 26.5cm) rectangles of black satin for the purse and purse lining. Cut a 12½ × 12in (32 × 30cm) rectangle of black satin for the purse pocket. Fuse heavy-weight interfacing onto the wrong side of all three rectangles.

2 Sew the strip of gold sequinned braid to the insertion lace along one long edge with a small zigzag. Cut the braid-and-lace strip into 11in (28cm) lengths and sew these together so that the lace and gold braid alternate. Sew a final 11in (28cm) length of insertion lace to the last strip of gold braid so that there is a strip of lace at each end. The lace and gold sequinned rectangle now measures 12½ × 11in (32 × 28cm).

4 Fold the black satin pocket piece in half lengthwise, wrong sides facing. Place the outer section of the purse lace side down, then pin and baste the pocket piece to the bottom half of it, raw edges even. Bind all four sides with black satin ribbon, mitering the corners.

3 Place the two smaller satin rectangles together, wrong sides facing. Lay the lace and sequin rectangle on top – the black satin will be visible through the lace. Pin and baste the three layers together. Trim off any excess lace and sequins. This forms the outer section of the purse.

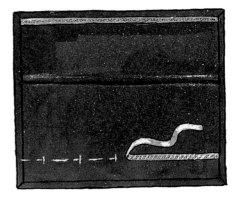

5 Fold the top flap of the purse over the pocket so that it covers all but the bottom 1½in (4cm). Use pins to mark on the pocket where the flap will be held closed. Slip stitch a Velcro strip underneath the top flap and along the line of marker pins on the pocket.

Variations & Tips
- Decorate the flap closure with a stylish gold button or a black braided tassel.
- Use different colored sequinned braid or satin to coordinate with a special evening outfit.

CLOTHING

"Anne took the dress and looked at it in reverent silence. Oh, how pretty it was — a lovely soft brown gloria with all the gloss of silk; a skirt with dainty frills and shirrings; a waist elaborately pintucked in the most fashionable way, with a little ruffle of filmy lace at the neck"

L.M. Montgomery, *Anne of Green Gables*

LACE TRIMS FOR BLOUSES

These are quick and easy ideas for making ready-to-wear blouses unique and special. For girlish frills and more sophisticated décolleté, lace adds that extra special touch.

GIRL'S BLOUSE

Materials
• *Ready-to-wear blouse with a Peter Pan collar and short puffed sleeves*
• *3yds (2.7m) of ½in (12mm) wide white edging lace*
• *1½yds (1.4m) of ⅛in (3mm) wide white entredeux*

Skill Level
Easy, 2 hours

LADY'S SHIRT

Materials
• *Ready-to-wear shirt with a pointed collar and a breast pocket*
• *1½yds (1.4m) of ½in (12mm) wide white Swiss insertion*

Skill Level
Easy, 2 hours

GIRL'S BLOUSE

1 Trim the fabric off one edge of the entredeux and sew gathered edging lace to it. Trim off the fabric on the other side of the entredeux and butt this up against the edges of the collar and sleeves.

2 Zigzag the entredeux to the collar and sleeves, making sure that the zigzag just catches the edge of the fabric. Zigzag the raw ends of lace together on the sleeves to neaten and trim off any excess lace and entredeux. Turn under the raw ends of lace on the collar and slip stitch to the neck or collar edge. You may have to overlap or narrow the ends of the lace on the collar to get a neat fit.

LADY'S SHIRT

1 Cut off the fabric edges on the Swiss insertion and pin it along the sleeve, pocket and collar edges, turning under a small hem at each end. On the collar, pin the outside edge first, form the miters at each corner and then pin the inner edges. Zigzag both edges in place. Zigzag along the raw ends of the Swiss insertion to hold the turned under hem in place.

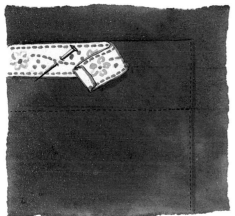

Variations & Tips

- The white Swiss insertion makes a strong contrast against the dark-colored fabric of the lady's shirt, but it also looks very pretty on pastel colors as well as white on white.

- Entredeux and gathered edging lace can also be used to trim square, round and puritan collars. It can also be zigzagged down the front of the blouse to give the effect of a "false" placket opening.

ROSEBUD COLLAR

*An exquisite detachable collar, designed as a series of
lace-trimmed scallops decorated with tiny rosebuds, provides
the finishing touch for a little girl's party dress.*

Materials

- ¼yd (25cm) of 36in (1m) wide white organdy
- 1¾yds (1.6m) of ⅜in (1cm) wide white insertion lace
- 3yds (2.7m) of ¾in (2cm) wide white edging lace
- 18in (46cm) strip of 1in (2.5cm) wide white bias binding
- Two small clear plastic snaps
- White embroidery thread

Templates

Collar scallop, page 124
Single rose embroidery design, page 121

Skill Level

Intermediate, 4–5 hours

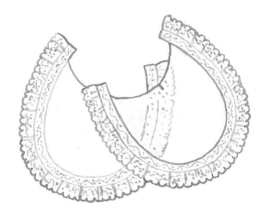

1 Cut six 5½in (14cm) squares of organdy. Pin the collar template to each square of organdy with the straight of grain line correctly positioned, and lightly trace around it with a pencil. Be sure to mark the center point of the neck edge on each fabric piece.

2 Pin the outer edge of a length of insertion lace around the curved pencil outline on each organdy square, leaving a ½in (12mm) tail of lace at each end. Shape the lace into the curve and stitch the inner edge of the lace to the organdy only. Unpin the outer edge and trim away the excess organdy.

3 Sew gathered edging lace to the other side of the insertion lace. Use an 18in (46cm) strip of lace for each collar piece, gathering the lace more fully around the bottom curve.

4 Lay the six collar pieces on a soft, flat surface such as a cushion or ironing board cover, and pin them in place starting from the left. Overlap each piece so that the outer edge of the insertion lace aligns with the center point marked on the piece underneath. The circle of the neck edge thus formed has a diameter of 3½in (9cm). Baste the pieces together at the neck edge and trim off the lace extensions.

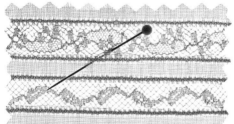

Variations & Tips

- Use batiste or voile instead of organdy. Pastel colors also look beautiful with white lace.
- Embroider the rosebuds with a colored thread to coordinate the collar with a special party dress.
- Use a gold beauty pin to fasten the collar at the back.

5 Bind the neck edge with the white bias binding. Place the collar around the wearer's neck and adjust to fit by overlapping the lace scallops as necessary. Stitch two snaps to the bias binding to close. Embroider a small white bullion rose on each of the points where the insertion laces of the collar pieces overlap.

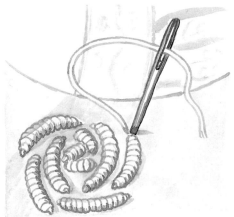

CAMISOLE AND HALF-SLIP

Treat yourself to gorgeous fabrics and beautiful laces with this luxurious camisole and half-slip set — in the Italian and French style but at a mere fraction of the price!

HALF-SLIP

Materials

- ¾yd (70cm) of 45in (115m) wide turquoise Swiss batiste or lawn
- 1¼yds (1.2m) of 2in (5cm) wide white Swiss insertion with a colorful floral embroidery design
- 3¾yds (3.4m) of ⅝in (2cm) wide white insertion lace
- 2½yds (2.3m) of 1½in (4cm) wide white edging lace
- 1yd (1m) of ¼in (6mm) wide white elastic

Skill Level

Easy, 2–3 hours

CAMISOLE

Materials

- Commercial pattern for a camisole
- 1yd (1m) of 45in (115cm) wide turquoise Swiss batiste or lawn
- ¾yd (70cm) of 2in (5cm) wide white Swiss insertion with a colorful floral embroidery design
- 1¼yds (1.2m) of ½in (12mm) wide white insertion lace
- 1¼yds (1.2m) of 1½in (4cm) wide white edging lace
- Water soluble marker pen

Templates

Chevron, page 122

Skill Level

Advanced, 8 hours

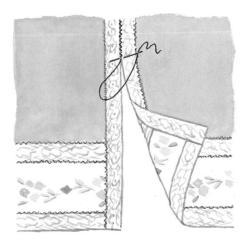

HALF-SLIP

1 Calculate the width of the required rectangle of Swiss batiste by adding 5in (12.5cm) to the hip measurement. Measure from the waist to above the knee and add 1in (2.5cm) for the waistband to find the length. Remember that the fancy band at the bottom hem will also add to the length.

2 Sew a strip of insertion lace to both sides of the embroidered Swiss insertion. Try to position the insertion laces so that the patterns match. Sew this lace band to one long edge of the batiste. Trim the ends of the lace band so that they are level with the fabric.

3 Cut two strips of insertion lace long enough to be sewn vertically down the sides of the batiste plus the lace band. Add an extra 2in (5cm) to allow for matching the lace designs. Sew in place, starting at the top edge of the fabric.

4 Sew the vertical insertion laces together, taking care to match the lace designs. Start at the top edge and finish 5½in (14cm) above the bottom edge, thus forming the front opening to allow for ease of movement when sitting and walking. Secure this seam with a couple of tiny back stitches. If you have matched the lace designs, both bottom edges of the lace band will remain level at the front opening.

5 Attach gathered edging lace to the bottom of the lace and embroidery band. Leave a ½in (12mm) tail of lace at each side of the front opening. Turn them under and slip stitch in place to neaten.

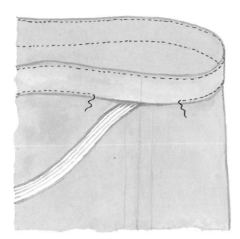

6 To make the casing for the elastic, press under a ¼in (6mm) seam, then a ½in (12mm) hem at the waist edge. Straight stitch along both the bottom and the top edges of this casing, leaving a 2in (5cm) opening along the bottom edge. Cut a piece of elastic that is 1in (2.5cm) larger than your waist measurement and insert it into the casing. Overlap the ends of the elastic by ½in (12mm) and sew them together. Hand stitch the opening closed.

CAMISOLE

1 Measure the widest part of the pattern for the front of the camisole and halve this measurement. Cut two rectangles of fabric to this width and to the length of the front pattern piece. Cut a strip of embroidered Swiss insertion the length of the camisole front and roll and whip the two pieces of fabric to either side of it.

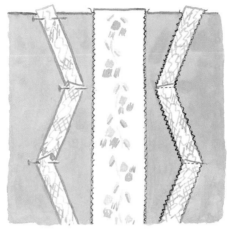

2 Sew two strips of insertion lace down the front of the camisole, one on either side of the embroidered Swiss insertion. Shape both strips of lace into the chevron design, mitering each angle.

3 Sew two rows of twin-needle pintucks alongside each of the lace chevrons, using the lace design as a guide. Draw a line extending out from each miter of the lace using a marker pen. Sew the first pintuck until the twin needles straddle the first bisecting line. With the needles in the down position, lift the presser foot and turn the fabric to achieve the required angle. Put the foot down and continue to the next miter. Repeat until all four pintucks are complete. Note that the needles will not break when you twist the fabric at each miter.

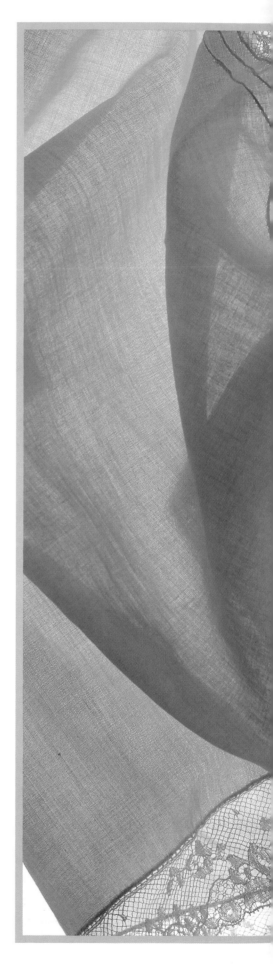

4 Cut the front of the camisole from the rectangle of lace and fabric you have just sewn, making sure that the center of the pattern front lies down the center of the Swiss insertion. Complete the rest of the camisole following the instructions on the pattern. Finally, sew gathered edging lace all around the lower edge of the camisole.

Variations & Tips
• To make a quicker version of the camisole, omit the lace and pintuck chevrons.
• Finish the neck and sleeves of the camisole with bias binding, extending it to form shoe-string shoulder straps.
• Sew an extra 8in (20cm) of lace band for the bottom of the half-slip and use it to make a matching potpourri sachet.

REGENCY NIGHTGOWN

*Inspired by Regency-style dresses, this nightgown is
both elegant and comfortable to wear. The skirt features
Regency stripes, insertion laces and Swiss embroideries.*

Materials

- *3yds (2.7m) of 45in (115cm) wide blue striped voile*
- *13¼yds (12m) of ⅜in (1cm) wide white insertion lace*
- *1½yds (1.4m) of ½in (12mm) wide white beading lace*
- *2¾yds (2.5m) of 1¼in (3cm) wide white edging lace*
- *1½yds (1.4m) of ⅜in (1cm) wide white edging lace*
- *1¼yds (1.2m) of ⅝in (1.5cm) wide white Swiss beading*
- *3yds (3m) of ⅜in (1cm) wide white double-sided satin ribbon*
- *1½yds (1.4m) of ¼in (6mm) wide white double-sided satin ribbon*
- *Two small clear plastic snaps*

Sizes

Small 32–34in (81–86cm)
Medium 36–38in (91–97cm)
Large 40–42in (102–107cm)
Length 51in (130cm)

Templates

Bodice front and back, page 124

Skill Level

Advanced, 10 hours

1 To make the skirt of the
nightgown, cut two pieces of
fabric measuring 45 × 39in
(115 × 100cm). The length of
39in (100cm) is from under the bust
to the ankle so adjust as necessary.
Remember, if you lengthen the skirt
of the nightgown you will need a
greater quantity of insertion lace
for the stripes.

2 Calculate where best to insert
the strips of lace. Here, the
stripes of the fabric are ½in (12mm)
wide and five strips of insertion lace
are sewn into each skirt piece at
7½in (19cm) intervals. The two
skirt pieces are also joined
together with strips of lace. The
finished circumference of the skirt
is 2½yds (2.3m).

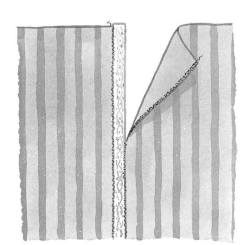

3 To insert the strips of lace, cut
the skirt lengthwise halfway
through a stripe. This creates two
¼in (6mm) seam allowances. Sew
the insertion lace to the fabric,
taking care to keep the top and
bottom edges even by pulling the
fabric toward you when sewing the

second side of each insertion strip.
When you reach the last strip of
insertion lace, do not sew the top
6in (15cm) on one edge. Instead,
roll and whip the fabric edge. This
will become the opening at the
center front of the skirt.

4 Trim the bottom and top
edges of the skirt so that they
are even, and sew gathered 1¼in
(3cm) wide edging lace around the
bottom of the skirt. Sew two rows
of gathering threads around the top
edge of the skirt, starting and
finishing on either side of the strip
of lace at the center front opening.

5 Cut out the back and two front
bodice pieces. Join the two front
pieces to the back at the shoulders
and sides with French seams. Cut
two 1½ × 23in (4 × 58cm) strips of
fabric on the bias and use these to
bind the armholes. Sew beading lace
up both front edges and around the
neck. Sew ⅜in (1cm) wide edging
lace to the beading. Do not gather
the edging lace when attaching it
to the beading.

6 Sew the Swiss beading along the bottom edge of the bodice, leaving a 1in (2.5cm) tail at each front edge. Turn under the tails, matching up the ribbon slots, and slip stitch in place. Gather the top of the skirt to fit the Swiss beading and sew in place.

7 Thread ³⁄₈in (1cm) wide ribbon through the Swiss beading under the bust, leaving long tails that can be tied attractively at the front. Overlap the front bodices and pin them together to mark where they fit most comfortably. Stitch two snaps to close the bodice in this position. Thread ¹⁄₄in (6mm) wide ribbon through the beading lace around the neck and adjust its length so that the neckline does not gape. Slip stitch the ribbon in place at the ends and the shoulder seams to stop it from twisting. Finally, tie the long tails of ribbon into a bow.

Variations & Tips
• Omit the lace insertion strips on the skirt and make a placket opening at the center front.
• Use contrasting colored ribbons to thread through the beadings and to bind the armholes.

KIMONO DRESSING GOWN

The use of lace and entredeux in this elegant gown is understatement itself. For those who think that lace is too fussy and frilly, let this dressing gown change your mind.

Materials
- 4½yds (4m) of 45in (115cm) wide plaid cotton fabric
- 11yds (10m) of ⅛in (3mm) wide white entredeux
- 1¾yds (1.6m) of ⅝in (1.5cm) wide white insertion lace

Size
Small 34–36in (86–91cm)
Medium 38–40in (97–102cm)
Large 42–44in (107–112cm)
Length 51in (130cm)

Templates
Front, back, pocket, sleeve, tie belt, neck band, sleeve band and pocket band – page 125
Large and small diamonds, page 124

Skill Level
Intermediate, 8–10 hours

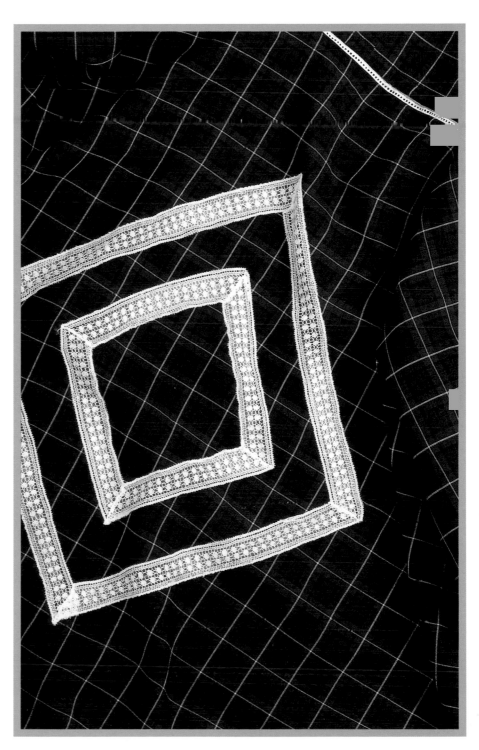

1 Cut out all the pattern pieces as shown on the cutting layout template. You will need one back, two fronts, two sleeves, two sleeve bands, two neck bands, one pocket, one pocket band and one tie belt. If you wish to make a shorter or longer gown, adjust the length of the fronts, back and neck bands.

2 Iron a crease down the center of the pocket and baste the small diamond outline onto it, centering the diamond along the fold. Iron a crease down the center of the back of the kimono and baste the large and small diamonds onto it, one inside the other. Position them so that the vertical points lie on the crease and the apex of the larger diamond is 3in (7.5cm) from the neck edge. Shape the three diamonds using insertion lace and sew them in place, cutting away the fabric from behind them.

3 The seams of the kimono are joined in the following order using entredeux. Sew entredeux to the front shoulder seams and then join the back piece to the fronts along the entredeux. Press a crease down the center of each sleeve and sew a strip of entredeux along the top edge of each sleeve. Align each crease with the shoulder seams, pin in place, then sew the kimono to the entredeux all along the top of the sleeves. Sew entredeux to the bottom edge of the sleeves, then sew the sleeve bands to the entredeux.

4 Sew a strip of entredeux to the side and sleeve seams of the front pieces in one continuous seam from the ends of the sleeve bands right around to the hem of the kimono. Join the side and sleeve seams of the back piece to this entredeux in one continuous seam.

5 Attach entredeux to the neck and front edges of the gown, starting at the hem of one of the front pieces and continuing around the neck edge and down to the hem on the other front piece. Sew the two neck bands together along one short side, right sides together and matching the plaid pattern. Press the seam open. Pin this seam at the center back and sew the neck band to the entredeux. Sew entredeux to the top edge of the pocket and then sew the pocket band to the entredeux.

6 Turn up ½in (12mm) and then a further 1¼in (3cm) along the bottom of the kimono and sew the hem in place. Turn under and press a ⅝in (1.5cm) fold along the neck, sleeve and pocket bands. Butt these folds up against the entredeux on the inside of the kimono and press in place. Pin and straight stitch all the bands in place.

7 Fold the belt in half lengthwise, right sides together, and straight stitch all three sides, leaving an opening of 4in (10cm) along the long edge. Trim the seams, clip the corners, and turn the belt right side out. Stitch the opening closed and press. Place the pocket on the right front side of the kimono, positioning it just below the tie belt. Using the lines of the plaid as a guide, straight stitch the pocket in place, turning under a tiny hem as you stitch.

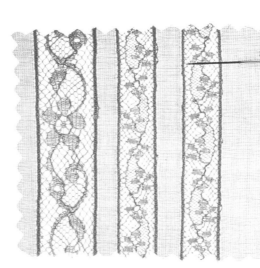

Variations & Tips

• Substitute French seams for the entredeux seams.

• Omit the lace diamonds and make a shorter version for a man.

• Choose a plaid with a small repeat pattern – the lines provide an excellent guide for cutting and sewing on the straight of grain.

BEADED EVENING BLOUSE

*Simple shape and design, combined with the beauty of
all-over lace, make this evening blouse a timeless classic.
The sparkling beads draw attention to the floral design.*

Materials

- *Commercial blouse pattern with
the following features: a round neck;
long straight sleeves with ease rather
than gathers across the top of the
sleeve; no darts except for a dart at
the bust line; side seams and a center
back seam only*
- *2¼yds (2m) of 36in (90cm) wide
double-edged black lace net*
- *¾yd (70cm) of black satin bias
binding*
- *11mm self-covering button*
- *Small round beads in gold, bronze,
copper, and opal*

Templates

Cutting layout, page 123

Skill Level

Easy, 8–10 hours plus beading time

1 To emphasize the beauty of the
lace design, eliminate as many
seams and hems as possible by
following the suggested cutting
layout. The lower hems of the
sleeves, front and back are removed
by utilizing the scalloped edge of the
lace. The center line of the back
pattern piece is placed on the fold of
fabric to eliminate any back seam.

2 Construct the blouse using tiny
French seams. First, sew the front
to the back at the shoulder seams.
Make a 6in (15cm) continuous
placket opening down the center
back using a 14in (36cm) strip of
the net lace. Finish the neck edge
with satin bias binding, neatening
and turning under the binding at the
left-side edge only.

3 Set in the sleeves, easing them in
gently across the top of the
shoulders. Too much gathered lace at
the top of the sleeve may spoil the
lace design. Sew the sleeve and side
seams in one continuous French
seam. Take care to match the lace
scallops at the hems on the sleeves
and side seams.

4 Cover the button with black
satin and stitch it onto the left
neck opening. Make a small button
loop from black satin, tuck the raw
edges inside the unfinished bias
binding on the right-side edge of
the neck and slip stitch in place.

5 Bead the scallops of the lace
design to add weight and help
the blouse hang more attractively.
Consider beading the centers, petals
or stamens of the flowers on the rest
of the lace. It is not necessary to
bead every flower but make sure that
the beading follows a regular pattern
and is not completely random.

Variations & Tips

• Use black satin bias binding to bind the center back opening.

• If you do not have the time to bead the lace blouse leave it plain, or buy pre-beaded lace, although this can be expensive.

• Wear a black- or cream-colored camisole underneath to display the lace design to best advantage.

EVENING SHAWL

*A truly luxurious accessory of finest silks and laces, this
shawl can be worn by mother and daughter for generations.
It is a perfect cover-up after a party or theater outing.*

Materials
- *33in (84cm) square of black
crepe de chine*
- *22½yds (20.5m) of 1¼in (3cm)
wide black insertion lace*
- *5¼yds (4.8m) of 5in (12.5cm)
wide black edging lace*

Templates
Log cabin square, page 123

Skill Level
Easy, 8–10 hours

1 Sew a strip of insertion lace to
each side of the square of crepe
de chine, overlapping the laces at the
corners in a log cabin design, as
shown on the template. To do this,
extend the lace strips beyond each
corner by approximately 2in (5cm),
then trim off any excess lace as close
to the zigzag stitching as possible
once the next strip has been
attached. Sew four more strips of
insertion lace to the first row, again
overlapping the laces at the corners.
Continue adding rows of lace until
you reach the size required. Here,
five rows of lace are used.

2 Attach the edging lace around
all four sides. Start stitching at a
corner, leaving a 6in (15cm) tail of
lace. Gently gather the lace to ease it
around the first three corners but do
not gather the lace along the sides.
Miter the final corner.

Variations & Tips
- Replace some or all of
the rows of insertion lace with a
wide strip of net lace.
- For a less expensive shawl,
increase the size of the crepe-de-
chine square and reduce the
number of rows of insertion lace.
- A summer daytime shawl will
look stunning in white or cream.

CHRISTMAS

"I have always thought of Christmas time ... as a good time; ... the only time I know of ... when men and women seem by one consent to open their shut-up hearts freely"

Charles Dickens, *A Christmas Carol*

CRACKERS AND TREE ORNAMENTS

With pretty lace snowflakes gleaming in the lights of the Christmas tree and sparkling party crackers for that extra touch of fun, the yuletide ambience will be complete.

CRACKERS

Materials (to make two crackers)

- *10 × 7in (25 × 18cm) rectangle of red silk douppioni*
- *10 × 7in (25 × 18cm) rectangle of green silk douppioni*
- *1yd (1m) of 1in (2.5cm) wide gold edging lace*
- *1yd (1m) of ½in (12mm) wide gold edging lace*
- *Two sequinned Christmas motifs*
- *Heavy-weight interfacing*
- *Two 6in (15cm) long cardboard tubes with a diameter of 1½in (4cm)*
- *Double-sided sticking tape*
- *1yd (1m) of gold metallic cord*

Skill Level

Easy, 1–2 hours

TREE ORNAMENTS

Materials

- *Small Battenburg lace motifs*
- *Fabric paints*
- *Sequins and beads*
- *Glitter glue*
- *Gold thread*

Skill Level

Easy, ½ hour per ornament

CRACKERS

1 Straight stitch the gold edging laces together so that the decorative edge of the 1in (2.5cm) wide lace slightly overlaps the straight edge of the ½in (12mm) wide lace. Cut this into four equal lengths. Sew a strip of this gold lace to each short side of the silk rectangles by zigzagging along the other side of the insertion lace. The edging should fan out slightly from the insertion.

2 Cut two rectangles of interfacing slightly smaller in size than the silk rectangles and iron them onto the wrong side of the silk. Wrap the silk rectangles around the cardboard tubes, overlapping the sides of the fabric. Tape the sides of the silk closed using double-sided tape. Whip stitch the ends of the gold lace together and trim off any excess.

3 Slide a small gift inside each tube. Check that the tubes are centrally positioned, then tie gold cord at each end. The cracker looks more attractive if the cord is not pulled too tightly. Using double-sided tape, stick a sequinned motif in the center of each tube.

TREE ORNAMENTS

1 Paint the lace motifs with fabric paint. Try using opalescent paint mixed with green, red, white and gold colors. Paint into the creases and folds of the motifs to get the best coverage. Allow to dry. The motifs are now stiff and firm.

2 Sew beads onto the motifs. Choose your own arrangement, such as along the edges of the shapes and in the centers. Squeeze glitter glue onto the surface of the motifs and press sequins into it.

3 Sew a length of gold thread through the motifs, tie the ends into a knot and hang the ornaments on the Christmas tree.

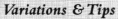

Variations & Tips

• The crackers not only make a special gift wrap for small gifts such as jewelry and perfume, but are also a charming way of giving money, book tokens, holiday or theater tickets.

• The tree ornaments are so easy to make that your children or grandchildren could make them with a little help from you.

FESTIVE TABLE SETTINGS

The simple design of these place mats and napkins will add a glamorous seasonal touch to the Christmas table. They can easily be varied for other special occasions too.

PLACE MATS

Materials (to make three mats)
- ½yd (50m) of 45in (115cm) wide red quilted fabric
- 5yds (4.6m) of ⅝in (1.5cm) wide red satin ribbon
- Three large white or green holly leaf Battenburg motifs

Skill Level
Easy, 1 hour

NAPKINS

Materials (to make three napkins)
- ½yd (50cm) of 45in (115cm) wide red cotton fabric
- Three large white or green holly leaf Battenburg motifs

Skill Level
Easy, 1 hour

PLACE MATS

1 To make the place mats, cut the red quilted fabric into three rectangles, each one measuring 17 × 12in (43 × 30cm).

2 In one of the corners of each rectangle, position and pin a Battenburg motif so that the widest points of the motifs touch the edges of the rectangles. The top of the motifs may extend beyond the corners of the rectangles and you will find that this enhances the design of the mats. Straight stitch the motifs in place, then using a close zigzag, sew over the straight stitching. Cut away the red quilted fabric from behind the motifs.

3 Bind the edges of the mats with red satin ribbon, mitering the binding at the corners.

NAPKINS

1 Cut three 15in (38cm) squares of red cotton fabric. Turn under and press a ¼in (6mm) hem along all four sides of each square. Turn under and press a second ¼in (6mm) hem and straight stitch in place. Attach the lace motifs in the same way as for the place mats.

Variations & Tips

• Make your own quilted fabric
by sandwiching a thin layer of
batting between two rectangles
of fabric. Stitch together with
a trellis of diagonal, wavy
or chevron lines.

• Sew a set of place mats and
napkins in colors that
complement your dinner set or
your dining room, or choose
different colors and motifs to suit
other festive occasions.

CHRISTMAS STOCKING

*Glittering gold lace, jewel-colored velvet and shimmering
silk make this stocking a rich tapestry of colors and
textures. Let your imagination run riot!*

Materials

- ½yd (50cm) of 45in (115cm) wide red silk douppioni
- Scraps of green velvet
- 4yds (3.7m) of gold edging lace in a variety of designs and widths
- ¼yd (25cm) of ¼in (6mm) wide red or gold ribbon
- 1½yds (1.4m) of piping cord
- Fray Check or similar product

Templates

Stocking, page 125

Skill Level

Easy, 5–6 hours

1 Cut out two stocking pieces from red silk. Seal the edges with Fray Check and allow to dry. Cut several 1½in (4cm) wide strips of red silk on the bias so that there is enough to make a 50in (1.3m) strip of piping cord. Sew the bias strips together, press the seams open and then press the strip in half lengthwise. Using a zipper or piping foot on your sewing machine, make the piping for the stocking.

3 Pin the piping to the right side of one of the stocking pieces, raw edges even and starting and stopping 1½in (4cm) from the top. Straight stitch in place. Pin the other stocking piece on top, right sides facing. Straight stitch them together along the same stitching line as the piping cord. Clip the seam around the curved edges on the "heel" and the "instep," then trim, turn right side out and press.

2 Cut up six irregular shapes from green velvet. Leaving the top 2½in (6cm) of the stocking empty, place the shapes at random on the front and back pieces. Pin them in position, then pin lengths of gold edging lace along each side of the velvet shapes (omit the topmost edge of velvet for the moment). To disguise the ends of the laces, start underneath another piece of lace or continue the lace so that it extends beyond the velvet shape to the edge of the stocking. Zigzag the lace in place. This will both stitch the lace in place and finish off the raw edges of the velvet. Zigzag the upper edge of the topmost piece of velvet to keep it firmly in place.

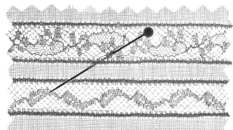

Variations & Tips

- For a more traditional look, use white lace instead of gold.
- Use scraps of any luxury fabrics in vibrant jewel colors instead of green velvet.

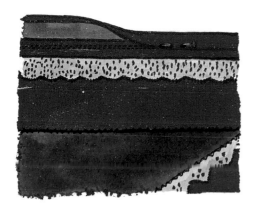

4 Pin a length of gold edging lace around the top edge of the stocking, 1in (2.5cm) down from the raw edge and leaving ½in (12mm) tails of lace at each end. Pin piping on top of the lace with the raw edge of the piping toward the top of the stocking. Straight stitch the piping and lace to the stocking. Turn over ⅛in (3mm), then another ⅜in (1cm) along the top of the stocking and press. Fold the hem over to enclose the raw edges of the piping. Press and stitch in place. Fold the hem back to the inside of the stocking, press and straight stitch in place, taking care not to catch the edging lace in the stitching.

5 Stitch two more rows of edging lace around the top of the stocking so that gold lace reaches from the piping to the first piece of velvet. Adding these strips of gold lace at the end makes finishing the top edge of the stocking easier. Zigzag the ends of the laces together and trim off any excess.

6 Finally, make a small loop by folding the ribbon in half and stitching it to the inside of the back seam of the stocking, underneath the piping. Now it is time to hang the stocking by your fireplace or mantel.

ANTIQUE LACE PILLOW

*The rich, festive color selected for this velvet pillow makes it
the perfect complement to a room decorated for Christmas –
a unique gift for friends or to grace your own hearth.*

Materials

- *Two equal lengths of wide antique Swiss edging – here, they are 18 × 7in (46 × 18cm)*
- *1½yds (1.4m) of 1½in (4cm) wide insertion lace in a color to match the Swiss edging – the exact length needed is determined by the quantity of Swiss edging available*
- *Sufficient red velvet to make a pillow on which to sew the antique lace – here, two 23 × 17½in (58 × 44cm) rectangles*
- *Batting*

Skill Level

Easy, 3–4 hours

1 The finished size of this pillow will be determined by the width and quantity of antique lace that you have available. Even a small quantity of antique lace, taken from a Victorian or Edwardian garment which is beyond repair, could make an eyecatching pillow for your sofa or bedroom.

2 Examine the Swiss edging for damage and choose two pieces of equal length. Do not be too fussy as slight imperfections on the lace can actually look very good. Wash and leave to dry. Join the long straight edges of the two pieces to a central strip of insertion lace.

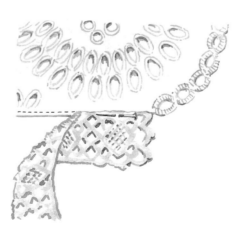

3 Turn under and press a tiny hem along the two raw edges of this lace rectangle. Stitch in place. Cut two more strips of insertion lace to the length of the neatened edges plus ½in (12mm). Turn under and stitch a ¼in (6mm) hem at the ends of the lace strips and straight stitch one to each neatened edge of the antique rectangle.

4 Pin out the finished rectangle on your ironing board, ensuring that the corners form right angles and that the sides are even in length. If the laces are delicate, spray with water and allow to dry naturally. Otherwise, steam and lightly press. Allow to dry.

5 Cut two rectangles of velvet to the size of the finished lace rectangle plus a 1in (2.5cm) seam allowance all around. Carefully position the antique lace rectangle on the center of one of the velvet rectangles. Pin along all four sides and down the center. Straight stitch the lace to the velvet, sewing along one of the seams on the central strip of insertion lace, and then all around the outside edge.

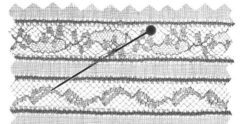

Variations & Tips

- Try to find lace with a decorative snowflake pattern.
- If you have antique lace with a leaf pattern, use it to make a Thanksgiving pillow.
- Make a series of different sized pillows – if they are very small, fill them with potpourri.

6 With right sides facing, sew the velvet rectangles together. Use the stitching line for the antique lace rectangle as a guide and straight stitch approximately ½in (12mm) outside of this. Leave a 6in (15cm) opening along one side. Turn the pillow right side out and check that the border of velvet around the lace rectangle is even on all four sides. Unpick and adjust if necessary. Fill the pillow with batting and slip stitch the opening closed.

TEMPLATES

Wherever possible, the templates have been shown full size. In these cases, simply trace or photocopy the template and then use as described in the main instructions. Sometimes, however, the templates have been reduced in size. In such instances, there are two options open to you. The first is to enlarge the template using a photocopier. To do this, set the photocopier to enlarge by the appropriate percentage, which is clearly indicated next to the template. The second option is to use the grid method. The templates are shown with a ⅜in (1cm) square grid over them. Next to each template you will find a ratio telling you what size grid you must redraw the template onto. Simply copy the lines of the template, square by square, onto the larger grid. For example, the interlacing rings below are shown at half their actual size. You must either set a photocopier to enlarge the template by 200% or redraw the shape onto a grid of ⅞in (2cm) squares.

General notes
CB indicates center back; **CF** indicates center front. Align the fold lines or **CB/CF** lines with the straight of grain on the fabric when cutting out; a double-headed arrow indicates the straight of grain where it may otherwise be unclear.

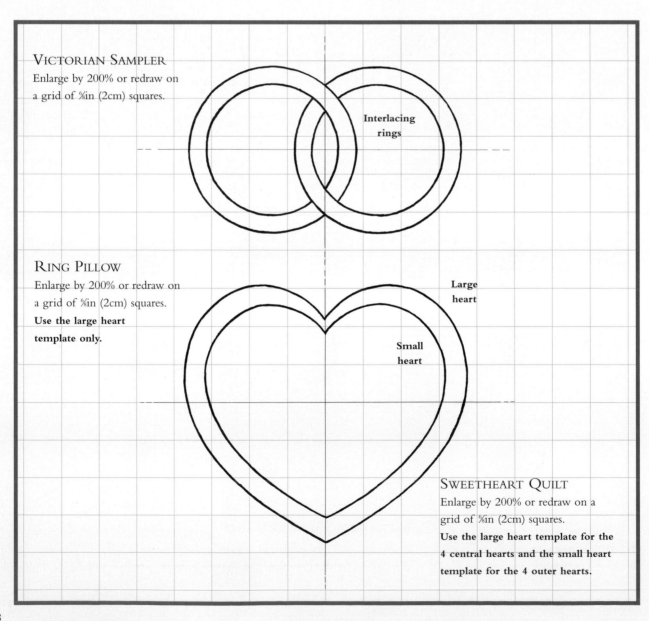

VICTORIAN SAMPLER
Enlarge by 200% or redraw on a grid of ⅞in (2cm) squares.

Interlacing rings

RING PILLOW
Enlarge by 200% or redraw on a grid of ⅞in (2cm) squares.
Use the large heart template only.

Large heart

Small heart

SWEETHEART QUILT
Enlarge by 200% or redraw on a grid of ⅞in (2cm) squares.
Use the large heart template for the 4 central hearts and the small heart template for the 4 outer hearts.

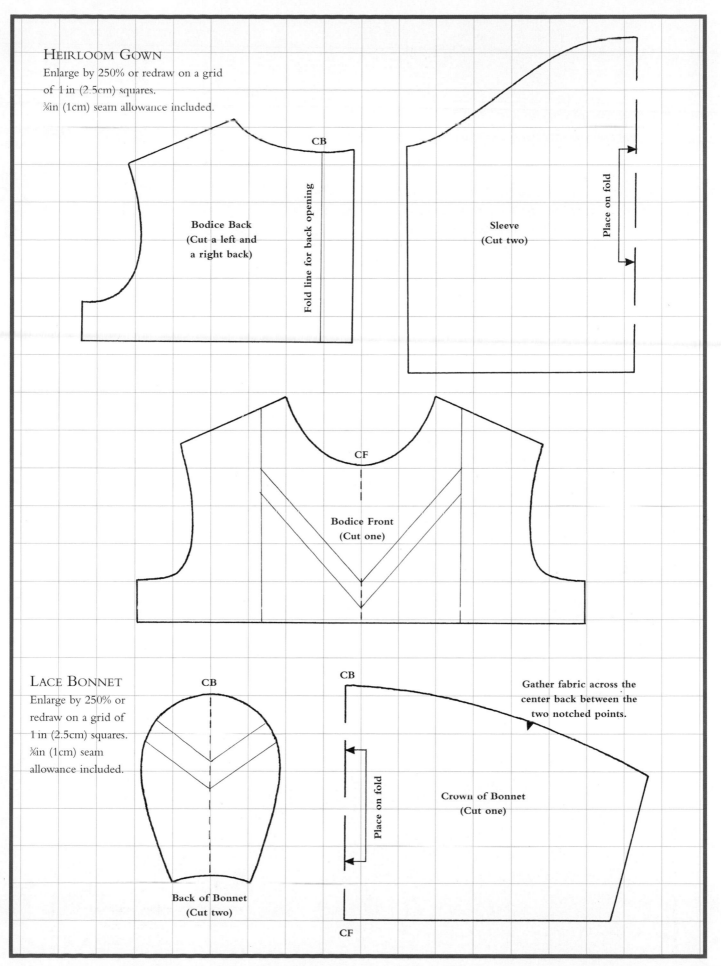

HEIRLOOM GOWN

Enlarge by 250% or redraw on a grid of 1 in (2.5cm) squares.

⅜in (1cm) seam allowance included.

CB

Bodice Back
(Cut a left and
a right back)

Fold line for back opening

Sleeve
(Cut two)

Place on fold

CF

Bodice Front
(Cut one)

LACE BONNET

Enlarge by 250% or redraw on a grid of 1 in (2.5cm) squares.

⅜in (1cm) seam allowance included.

CB

CB

Gather fabric across the
center back between the
two notched points.

Place on fold

Crown of Bonnet
(Cut one)

Back of Bonnet
(Cut two)

CF

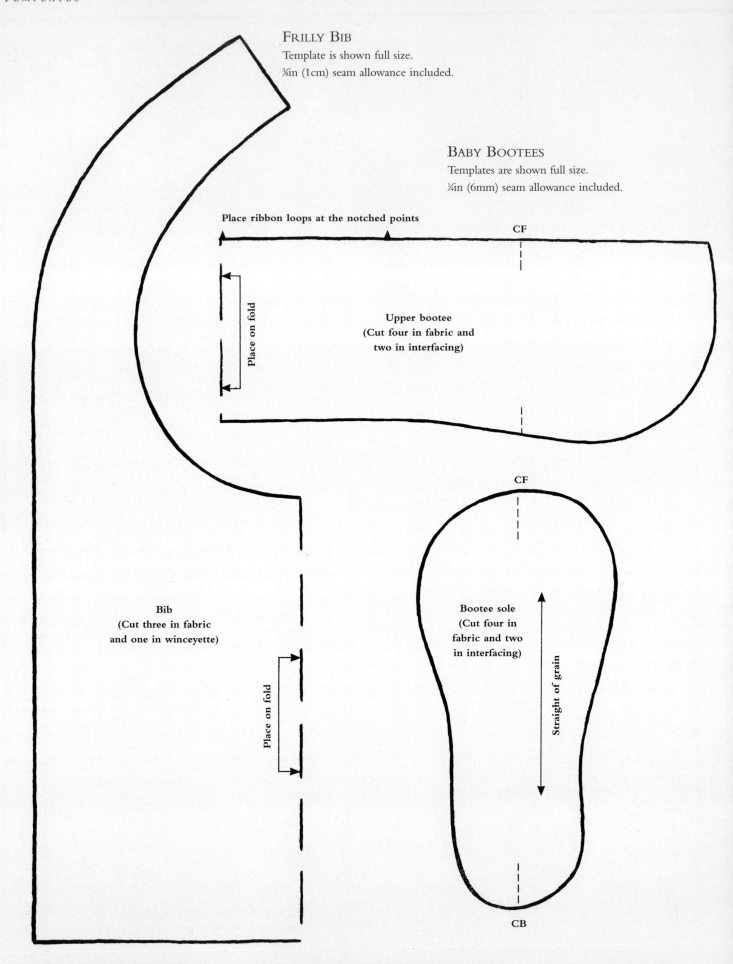

FRILLY BIB
Template is shown full size.
⅜in (1cm) seam allowance included.

BABY BOOTEES
Templates are shown full size.
¼in (6mm) seam allowance included.

Place ribbon loops at the notched points

CF

Place on fold

Upper bootee
(Cut four in fabric and
two in interfacing)

CF

Bib
(Cut three in fabric
and one in winceyette)

Bootee sole
(Cut four in
fabric and two
in interfacing)

Straight of grain

Place on fold

CB

EMBROIDERY DESIGNS

All templates are shown full size except for the floral trail design. Each of the stitches requires one strand of the appropriate colored embroidery thread (recommended colors and the corresponding DMC color codes are given in brackets).

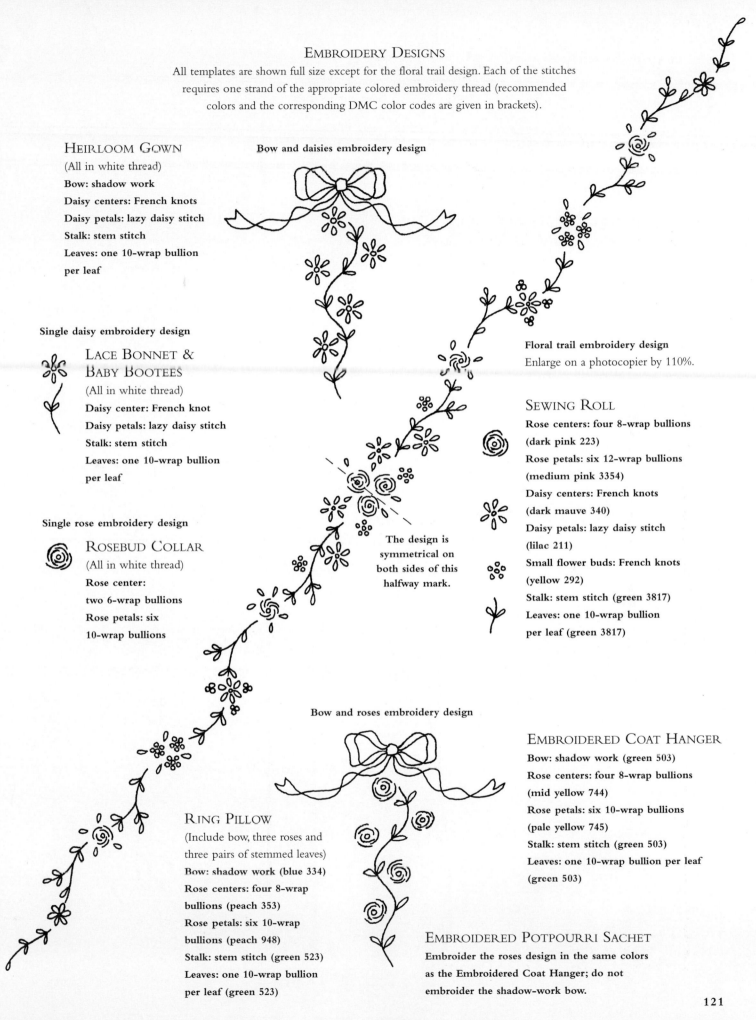

HEIRLOOM GOWN

(All in white thread)

Bow: shadow work

Daisy centers: French knots

Daisy petals: lazy daisy stitch

Stalk: stem stitch

Leaves: one 10-wrap bullion per leaf

Bow and daisies embroidery design

Single daisy embroidery design

LACE BONNET & BABY BOOTEES

(All in white thread)

Daisy center: French knot

Daisy petals: lazy daisy stitch

Stalk: stem stitch

Leaves: one 10-wrap bullion per leaf

Single rose embroidery design

ROSEBUD COLLAR

(All in white thread)

Rose center: two 6-wrap bullions

Rose petals: six 10-wrap bullions

Floral trail embroidery design
Enlarge on a photocopier by 110%.

SEWING ROLL

Rose centers: four 8-wrap bullions (dark pink 223)

Rose petals: six 12-wrap bullions (medium pink 3354)

Daisy centers: French knots (dark mauve 340)

Daisy petals: lazy daisy stitch (lilac 211)

Small flower buds: French knots (yellow 292)

Stalk: stem stitch (green 3817)

Leaves: one 10-wrap bullion per leaf (green 3817)

The design is symmetrical on both sides of this halfway mark.

Bow and roses embroidery design

RING PILLOW

(Include bow, three roses and three pairs of stemmed leaves)

Bow: shadow work (blue 334)

Rose centers: four 8-wrap bullions (peach 353)

Rose petals: six 10-wrap bullions (peach 948)

Stalk: stem stitch (green 523)

Leaves: one 10-wrap bullion per leaf (green 523)

EMBROIDERED COAT HANGER

Bow: shadow work (green 503)

Rose centers: four 8-wrap bullions (mid yellow 744)

Rose petals: six 10-wrap bullions (pale yellow 745)

Stalk: stem stitch (green 503)

Leaves: one 10-wrap bullion per leaf (green 503)

EMBROIDERED POTPOURRI SACHET

Embroider the roses design in the same colors as the Embroidered Coat Hanger; do not embroider the shadow-work bow.

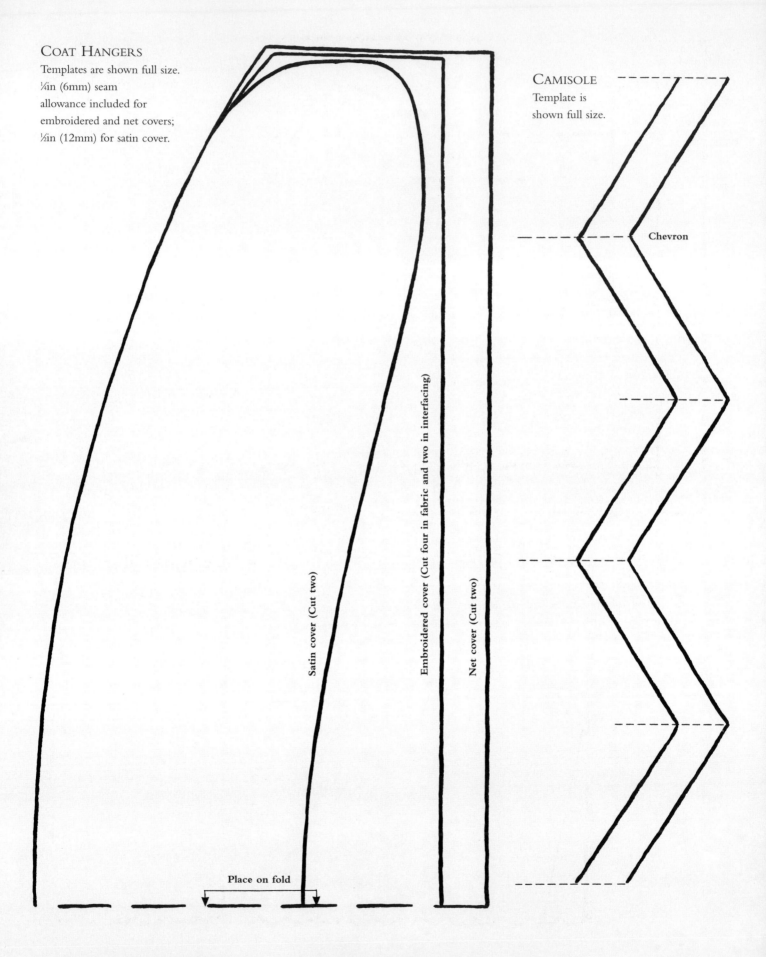

COAT HANGERS

Templates are shown full size.
¼in (6mm) seam
allowance included for
embroidered and net covers;
½in (12mm) for satin cover.

CAMISOLE

Template is
shown full size.

Chevron

Satin cover (Cut two)

Embroidered cover (Cut four in fabric and two in interfacing)

Net cover (Cut two)

Place on fold

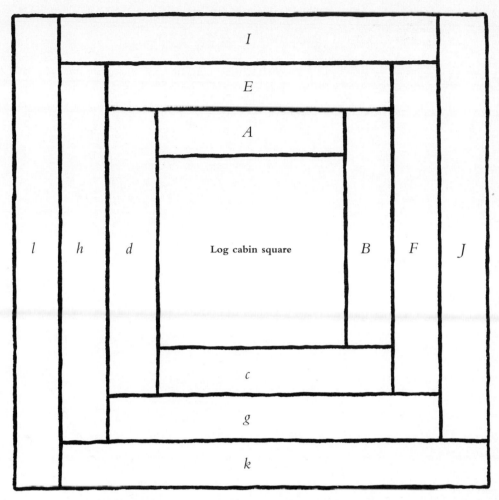

LOG CABIN PINCUSHION

Template is shown full size.

Attach strips of lace following the alphabetical order, using one lace design for all capital letters and the other for all lower case letters. Cut each strip of lace 1in (2.5cm) longer than shown here to allow for the corner joins.

EVENING SHAWL

Use the template as a guide for the corner joins only; do not use it as a size guide. Follow the instructions within the project for sizes.

BEADED EVENING BLOUSE

½in (1.5cm) seam allowance recommended for the French seams. **Use the template as a cutting layout only; it is not intended to be used as pattern pieces.**

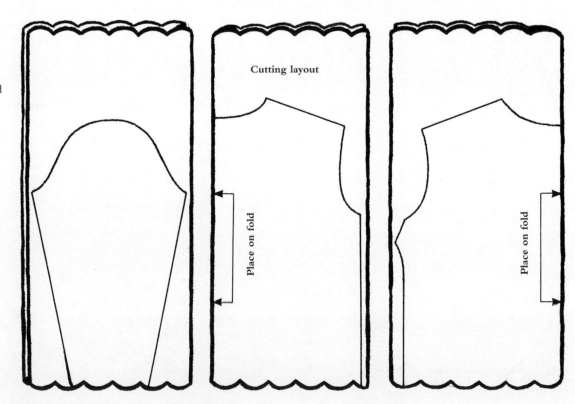

Cutting layout

Place on fold

Place on fold

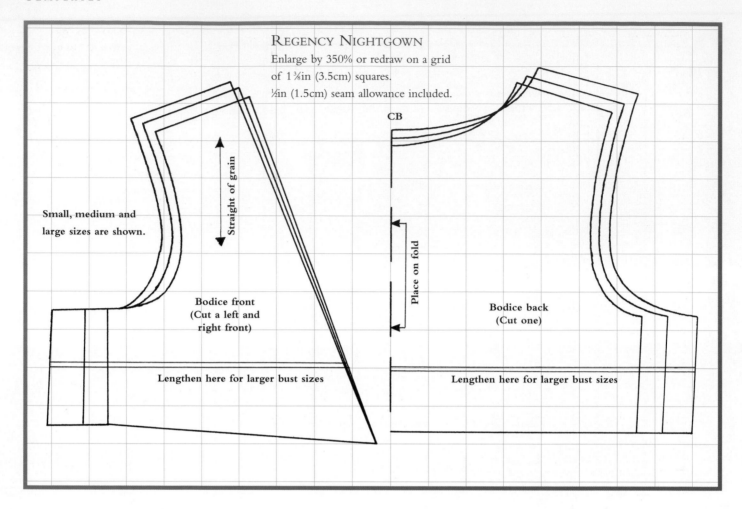

REGENCY NIGHTGOWN

Enlarge by 350% or redraw on a grid
of 1⅜in (3.5cm) squares.
½in (1.5cm) seam allowance included.

Small, medium and
large sizes are shown.

Straight of grain

CB

Place on fold

Bodice front
(Cut a left and
right front)

Bodice back
(Cut one)

Lengthen here for larger bust sizes

Lengthen here for larger bust sizes

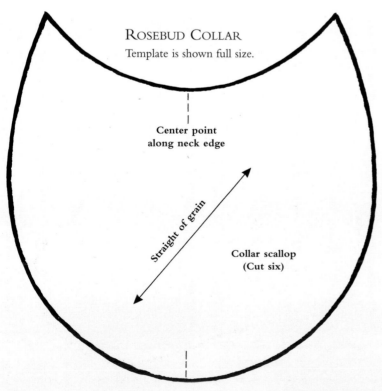

ROSEBUD COLLAR

Template is shown full size.

Center point
along neck edge

Straight of grain

Collar scallop
(Cut six)

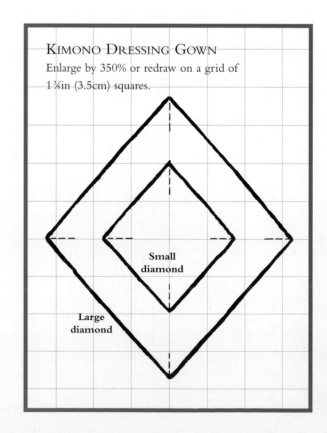

KIMONO DRESSING GOWN

Enlarge by 350% or redraw on a grid of
1⅜in (3.5cm) squares.

Small
diamond

Large
diamond

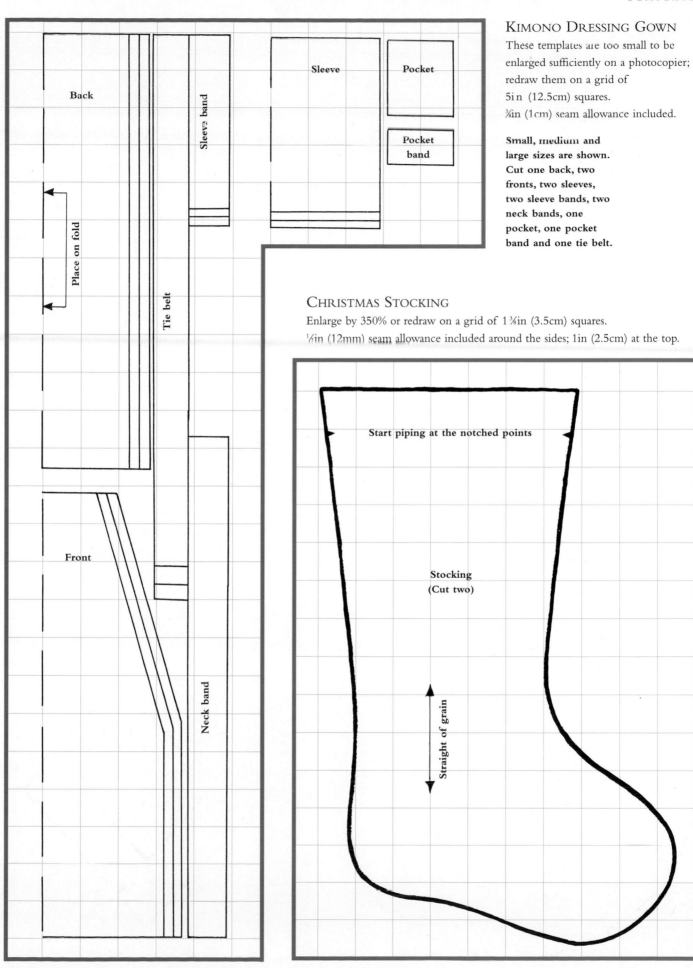

Back

Place on fold

Sleeve band

Tie belt

Sleeve

Pocket

Pocket band

Front

Neck band

KIMONO DRESSING GOWN

These templates are too small to be enlarged sufficiently on a photocopier; redraw them on a grid of 5in (12.5cm) squares. ⅜in (1cm) seam allowance included.

Small, medium and large sizes are shown. Cut one back, two fronts, two sleeves, two sleeve bands, two neck bands, one pocket, one pocket band and one tie belt.

CHRISTMAS STOCKING

Enlarge by 350% or redraw on a grid of 1⅜in (3.5cm) squares. ½in (12mm) seam allowance included around the sides; 1in (2.5cm) at the top.

Start piping at the notched points

Stocking (Cut two)

Straight of grain

INDEX

CREDITS

Author's acknowledgment

While writing this book I have been greatly helped by my friend Sarah Deem, the results of whose exquisite needlework, design skills, and professionalism can be seen on a number of projects in this book, in particular, the Christening ensemble, which is truly a work of art. Thank you, Sarah. My sister, Julie Gahan, has also given generously of her time, skills, knowledge, and creativity. Thank you for your support, Julie.

Suppliers

Binney & Smith Inc.
PO Box 431
Easton
PA 18044-0431
Tel: (US) 610 253 6271
Fax: (US) 610 250 5768
Liquitex fabric paints

DMC Creative World Ltd
Pullman Road
Wigston
Leicestershire LE18 2DY
Tel: (UK) 0116 281 1040
Fax: (UK) 0116 281 3592
Embroidery threads, Perle No. 5

Sarah Deem
16 Hungerford Road
Lower Weston
Bath BA1 3BU
Tel: (UK) 01225 339294
Traditional Christening robes

Expo International Inc.
5631 Braxton Drive
Houston
TX 77036-2105
Tel: (US) 713 782 6600
Fax: (US) 800 772 7545
All-over lace, lace motifs, gold lace

Ginny's Heirlooms
56 Park House Gardens
East Twickenham TW1 2DE
Tel & Fax: (UK) 0181 892 3246
Fabrics, cotton laces, Swiss embroideries

Handler Textile Corp
450 Seventh Avenue
New York
NY 10123
Tel: (US) 212 695 0990
Fax: (US) 212 695 1496
Interfacings, picture frame kits

Liberty
210-220 Regent Street
Westminster
London W1R 6AH
Tel: (UK) 0171 734 1234
Fax: (UK) 0171 573 9876
Floral print fabric

Lydia's
900 Bob Wallace Avenue #104
Huntsville
AL 35801
Tel: (US) 205 536 9700
Laces, fabrics

Martha Pullen Co.
518 Madison Street
Huntsville
AL 35801
Tel: (US) 205 533 9586
Fax: (US) 205 533 9630
Fabrics, laces

Newey Goodman Ltd
Sedgley Road West
Tipton
West Midlands DY4 8AH
Tel: (UK) 0121 522 2500
Fax: (UK) 0121 522 2299
Fray Check

Turnstyle
J.M. Jackson
Aistons
Preston Wyne
Hereford HR1 3PA
Tel: (UK) 01432 820505
Wooden Victorian reproduction pincushion

Wimpole Street Creations
PO Box 395
West Bountiful
UT 84087
Tel: (US) 801 298 0504
Fax: (US) 801 298 1333
Battenburg motifs, sequinned motifs